HIGH PRAISE FOR

BY PHIL MARCADE

MARCADE'S GREAT SENSE FOR STORYTELLING, as well as his knack for being in the right place at the right time, make this a must-read for those interested in the history of punk.
—LIBRARY JOURNAL

A MUSICIAN'S MEMOIR OF PUNK ROCK in its New York City heyday shows how much fun it was while it lasted, before AIDS and heroin had the last laugh. . . A must-read for those who love that era and want a fresh perspective on it.
—KIRKUS REVIEWS

IT WAS HARD TO PUT THIS BOOK DOWN. A fun and dishy read! . . . Gives us the real 411 about both CBGB's and Max's Kansas City and the drug scene that was happening.
—PUNK GLOBE

A FAST, FUN READ THAT FILLS IN historical gaps and establishes Phil Marcade as more than a character lurking in the shadows. Fans of CBGB and American punk will dig it.
—RAZORCAKE

MARCADE DETAILS A LIFE CONSUMED with rock & roll, and his arrival in New York from France at a time when The New York Dolls were new and igniting the wave of bands that tried to follow in their footprints.
—GOOD TIMES

GET IT! It's great!
—VICE

A COMPELLING ACCOUNT OF LIFE as an artistic Parisian in Downtown New York, back in the good/bad ol' days of sex and drugs and rock n roll. In a subculture of anti-fashion and nihilism, Marcade stood out with an urbane, sophisticated sound and style deeply rooted in R&B musicology—that makes sense now more than ever. *Vive La Revolution!*
—STEVEN BLUSH, AUTHOR/FILMMAKER,
NEW YORK ROCK, AMERICAN HARDCORE

AN INCREDIBLE INSIDER'S JOURNEY through New York's 1970s underground music scene. . . . From the hallways of the Chelsea Hotel to psychedelic barges on the canals of Amsterdam, from wild cross-country tours with his band The Senders to backstage antics at CBGB and Max's Kansas City, to the notoriously deadly dope houses of the Lower East Side, he experienced it all . . . and lived to tell. . . . A must-read for anyone interested in a behind-the-scenes glimpse into the nascent Manhattan punk scene . . . or American rock 'n' roll history.

—PLEASANT GEHMAN, AUTHOR, SHOWGIRL CONFIDENTIAL

JUST WHEN YOU THINK YOU LED a fascinating, fun, wild, scary life, along comes this maniac. I'm amazed Phil's still here. But thankful he managed to make it back with these untoppable tales from the inside of the inside—of his pals Johnny Thunders, Joe Strummer, Debbie Harry, Dee Dee Ramone, of Max's, CBs and the long-ago Lower East Side, all told in a matter-of-fact style that only makes them more incredible. A definitive dispatch from the trenches (and gutters) of New York punk.

—ROBERT DUNCAN, MANAGING EDITOR, CREEM;
AUTHOR, THE NOISE

A RIVETING ACCOUNT OF DESPERATE DAYS and high-octane nights that vividly recall the gritty glamour of New York in the 1980s, that penniless yet golden age of sex not sexting, drugs not hugs, and pure, unadulterated rock and roll. Written in blood by somebody who was there, in the combat zone, loving every manic minute.

—MAX BLAGG, POET

ONE OF THE GREATEST VIEWS OF NYC'S golden age you will ever find . . . from the leader of one of the greatest unheralded bands ever—The Senders. We see rockers, junkies, punks, dealers, poets, street characters stripped of their myth and experienced as they really were. Marcade's book is historically important, invaluable in fact, but it's also a fun, fast, nasty read.

—JAMES "THE HOUND" MARSHALL, BAR OWNER, RADIO
PERSONALITY, COLLECTOR, HISTORIAN, NEW YORKER

PHIL'S MEMOIR OF NYC in the 70s is almost as much fun as being there.

—PETER CROWLEY, MANAGER/BOOKING AGENT,
MAX'S KANSAS CITY

FEELS LIKE HAVING A CHAT with an old friend, remembering and laughing over those crazy, glorious times.

—IDA S. LANGSAM, RAMONES' PUBLICIST

PUNK AVENUE

PUNK AVENUE

inside the new york city underground 1972–1982

by Phil Marcade

THREE ROOMS PRESS

New York, NY

Punk Avenue: Inside the New York City Underground 1972–1982
by Phil Marcade

This is a work of creative nonfiction. The events are portrayed to the best of author Phil Marcade's memory. Some parts of this book, including dialog, characters and their characteristics, locations and time, may not be entirely factual.

ISBN 978-1-941110-49-2 (trade paperback)
ISBN 978-1-941110-50-8 (ebook)
Library of Congress Control Number: 2016955388

Originally published in French as *Au delà de l'avenue D* by Philipe Marcadé (Scali, August, 2007, 978-2350121765; Camion Blanc, November 2009, 978-2357790490). Translated by the author.

First Printing

COVER AND BOOK DESIGN:
KG Design International: www.katgeorges.com

FRONT COVER PHOTO:
"Steve Shevlin, Johnny Thunders, and Phil Marcade, 1979"
© Photo by Marcia Resnick: www.marciaresnick.com

PHOTO, PAGE 118
"Phil Marcade and Stiv Bators at CBGB, June 1978"
© Photo by Eileen Polk

DISTRIBUTED BY:
Publishers Group West: www.pgw.com

Printed in the United States of America
Three Rooms Press
561 Hudson Street, #33,
New York, NY 10014
threeroomspress.com
info@threeroomspress.com

10 9 8 7 6 5 4 3 2 1

For Pierre

A man is a success if he gets up in the morning
and gets to bed at night,
and in between, does what he wants to do.

—Bob Dylan

All my friends are dead,
or else they're not feeling too good.

—Tom Waits

PREFACE

Why were the seventies so important and interesting? Probably because nobody cared. There wasn't much money involved, there was no Internet, New York City was no man's land, and the terrorists were blowing up things all over Europe. Meanwhile, we were trying to play music that very few people were interested in hearing, so much the better. By the time the labels got interested, the best part was over.

Chris and I met Philippe in New York at CBGB's. He was the prettiest thing and his French accent was so intense I was embarrassed to ask him to repeat things because I couldn't understand him. He played and sang and looked great on stage.

We finally had a show together booked in a small theater on Eighth Avenue, which is now dedicated to dance shows. We asked him to translate "Denis" for me to sing the song in French, not knowing the full history of the Sylvie Vartan version. On that same day, there was a truly ridiculous scene created by a madman we once had for a manager and the owner of the theater. They were acting more punk than any of us and came to blows outside in front of the theater.

So Philippe and I never got to play that show together, but we got a really sweet translation of "Denis Denis."

—Debbie Harry

FOREWORD

If I ever was going to direct a movie of *Please Kill Me*, the book Gillian McCain and I did, I would put Philippe Marcade in the background of every scene, giggling with some exotic French beauty—just like in real life.

Philippe Marcade, while not a household name, was friends with everyone at CBGB and Max's Kansas City, and a bona fide member, in good-standing—of the New York Punk Rock Scene. Of course, there were only about two hundred in the beginning. John Holmstrom and I were relative latecomers on the scene, when we launched *Punk* magazine, and Philippe was already hanging out with the cool kids—Johnny Thunders, Richard Hell, and Dee Dee Ramone. And later, Stiv Bators, Sid Vicious, and Nancy Spungen.

I can't really speak to Philippe's musical abilities—despite what you might have read, I'm not a rock critic. I'm a pop culture historian, but I know what I like—and The Senders were great. Beyond that, I don't know anything about them. I can't tell you who was in the band, because Philippe was the only one I ever watched. He was a star, back in the day when that word meant something. Of course, nowadays, everyone is a star, so the word has lost all meaning. I'm using the original meaning of the word "star," when it meant fascinating, brilliant, and gorgeous.

Philippe was one of those guys my eyes went to—in a room full of stars: Debbie Harry, Iggy Pop, Patti Smith, and Joey Ramone. He was always at the right table or the perfect backstage scene, saying the right stuff with that thick French accent.

Don't get me wrong, like most Americans, I hate the French, but if everyone in France was like Philippe Marcade, I would move there tomorrow.

You see, Philippe Marcade was cool, when that word meant that you wanted to be sitting at his table, laughing along with all the cool people to Philippe's latest joke.

He was always dressed right, had the right words, the best hair, and like I said—the best skinny, top-shelf French model hanging on to his arm.

When Gillian and I wrote *Please Kill Me*, it was our hope that it would inspire kids around the world to document and record their own twisted lives. I know now that we have succeeded, because if we could inspire a deadbeat like Philippe to write a book, we can do anything!

Seriously.

When I started assembling the list of people to interview for *Please Kill Me*, Philppe was at the top of the list, just because I wanted to know what was going through his head during the punk days.

I was probably thinking, "Is Philippe really that cool?"

The answer, of course, is yes—otherwise you wouldn't even be reading this, moron.

His interview was even better than I expected. Philippe was just so damn funny. Philippe is one of the reasons doing the book was so much fun. It's so great to sit down and ask someone I've known—since I was eighteen years old—what they were thinking and what they remember, twenty years after the fact.

More people should do it, because it's very therapeutic.

I think it's also important to tell people what you think of them before they shuffle off this mortal coil. Thank God I got tell Joey, Dee Dee, and Johnny Ramone what I thought of them before they all died.

Interviewing people I've known for so long is great, because I usually find out that they were even more special than I thought.

One last note: if anyone out there is ever thinking about doing an oral history, and you want to make it good and funny, you need to talk to funny people. The reason so many people like *Please Kill Me* is because of all those lesser-known names like Jeff Mangum, Bob

Quine, and Philippe Marcade, who were mainstays on the scene—and so hysterically funny in real life.

Funny is more important than one might think and gets us all through the day.

Philippe also paid me the greatest compliment when I ran into him a couple of weeks after we did the interview.

Philippe told me that after talking about punk for a few hours, he appropriated that talk in his everyday life, which led to him telling his boss, "Fuck off!"

And his girlfriend.

And his bandmates.

And his mother, for all I know.

What was even better, is that Philippe was laughing hysterically when he told me.

Yeah, I know, cool.

—Legs McNeil

PUNK AVENUE

Phil, 1972

HAPPY BIRTHDAY TO YOU

Phoenix, November 1972

FOR MY EIGHTEENTH BIRTHDAY, I WAS transferred from the juvenile detention center in Phoenix, Arizona, to the federal penitentiary in Florence, Arizona.

In the car, handcuffs on my wrists, I asked the cop behind the wheel how long I was going to have to stay in *that* jail.

"That's gonna be for the judge to tell you, kid, but you can bet your ass it'll be at least five years," he said, laughing.

Five years in jail. It was with that in mind that I walked into the prison's main building, where I was told to strip before being searched butt naked, then sprayed from head to toe with lice killer. Pointing out that I didn't have lice didn't turn out to be such a good idea.

"From now on you only speak when a guard asks you something," that fat sweaty pig told me before spraying me right in the face with his fucking powder.

"From now on your name is 419031 and you better remember it if you're called," said the other creep at the counter where I got my uniform: jeans, a pair of white socks, white underwear, white sneakers, and a gray T-shirt with my new name, 419031, printed across the back.

Then, escorted by two armed guards, I had to walk down this long corridor in front of all the cells where my new neighbors, most of them heavily tattooed Mexican murderers, were held. I only got a few steps down that hellish hallway before they all started screaming, "*She's mine!*" "*Hey, bitch, you my new whore?*" and other such warm greetings.

Though I'd turned eighteen that very day, I looked more like fifteen. I wasn't shaving yet, had hair down to the middle of my back, and my face was covered with white lice-killer powder. They liked me.

I'm dead meat, I told myself, trying to keep my fear from showing too much. Fortunately, I got locked up some distance from those friendly fellows, in a large dormitory with about thirty losers who weren't quite as dangerous. That's where they kept guys who hadn't been sentenced yet, which meant they were all on their best behavior, hoping to improve their fates.

The non-sentenced block. Thank God!

As soon as the huge automatic metal door shut behind me, I heard a familiar voice call me by my old name:

"Philippe?"

It was Bruce, my traveling companion. We'd been busted together a week earlier.

"Bruce! It's so great to see you," I shouted out, at the last second holding myself back from taking him into my arms. Maybe this wasn't quite the right time. . . .

I had met Bruce eight months earlier in Holland, where I was hanging out instead of attending my drawing classes at the Academie Des Beaux-Arts in Paris, where I grew up.

Bruce, an American of Italian descent, always wore white shirts with the collar buttoned up all neat. He was six years older than me, had very long hair, and had already graduated from Boston University where— thanks to his grades, popularity, and unbeatable stamina—he'd been elected Student Body President, a title usually reserved for future prominent lawyers, judges, or presidents of the United States.

He had just finished crossing Europe on a motorcycle with a head full of dreams and a back pocket full of acid, when I met him, under the pouring rain, on the steps of the Paradiso in Amsterdam. He turned me onto one of his little pills, some Orange Sunshine, and we spent the following weeks watching raindrops exploding into rainbows on the pavement of the old port, listening to *After the Gold Rush*. Bruce lived with a Dutch girl named Marion, though he spent most of his time fucking a German girl named Astrid.

He came back to Paris with me. I put him up in my room where we spent most of our evenings smoking hash, listening to records, dreaming of adventures, and

eating the hundreds of strawberries and cherries that
we stole, by the crate-load, from the sidewalks in front
of the neighborhood grocery stores at five in the
morning, stoned out of our minds.

You could never be bored with Bruce. He was completely unpredictable.

One day, for example, we were peacefully walking
down the Boulevard Montparnasse when he suddenly
walked into a beauty parlor, snatched a blond wig from
the head of a mannequin in the window, and came
right back out laughing his ass off and with the huge
barber chasing after him. Fortunately, we were faster
than he was, and he gave up on us after a few blocks,
completely out of breath. The wig ended up on a skull
we stole from the catacombs at Denfert-Rochereau.

We were tripping on acid almost every night in
Paris—like the time we went to see T. Rex and ended
up in the meatpacking district at Les Halles at 5 a.m.
With our getups, we were not well received. It started
with one over-excited butcher throwing a piece of meat
at the back of my head and it got worse from there. We
had to run like hell as about fifty of them started bom-
barding us with chunks of meat. It was flying in all
directions and was terrifying—especially on acid.
Suddenly escaped from that hell, we decided to step
into Notre Dame. It was still early in the morning and
the cathedral was completely empty. Bruce must have
thought he was the Pope, because he decided to go sit

in the huge throne on the main center stage. This must have been strictly forbidden, as we were run out of there too—this time by an old priest, mad as hell. But at least he wasn't throwing chunks of meat at us.

In July, Bruce decided to go back to the States, and he invited me to come along. He arranged it so that his dad took me on as a student au pair, meaning I could get a visa. My parents, always cool, paid for the plane ticket to make me happy, although they probably weren't thrilled with the idea of their seventeen-year-old son leaving for the States with some hippie freak, without even having graduated from college.

I'd never been on a plane before, so that alone was exciting.

Of course, once in Boston, we didn't stay at Bruce's dad's for more than five minutes. Instead, we bought a badly beat-up Ford Econoline van from a Hare Krishna for a hundred bucks. We equipped it with an eight-track tape deck in the front and a huge mattress in the back, and we hit the road, the big one: Route 66. We were beside ourselves to be starting our grand adventure, our epic journey, our Easy Rider by van.

I couldn't believe it. "California, here I come!"

First we went up north, to Maine then New Hampshire, passing by the mountains of Franconia where Bruce had a splendid idea.

"We could climb up a mountain while smoking joints and watch the sun go down once we get to the top."

Why not?

After an hour or so of relatively easy climbing, it suddenly became much harder. We'd already gotten quite a ways up when we found ourselves at the foot of this huge cliff. We should have stopped there, but after smoking another joint, we decided to keep going. We figured once we made it to top of the cliff, we'd be on top of the mountain (super cool), and once up there we'd be able to find an easier way back down. Yeah, right.

I went first. Grasping the cracks of a near-vertical rock wall, we slowly made our way up. We must have been about halfway up the cliff when suddenly it all went wrong. A few feet below me, Bruce was starting to panic. He was drenched in sweat and shaking like a leaf.

"Holy shit, I'm gonna let go. I can't go up or down, I'm losing my grip." Below him, the big void. . . . It was terrifying.

Just above me, I saw a little niche in the rock, and I climbed in and sat, trying to figure out the best way to get back down to help him. I was starting to sweat now, too. I was wearing sneakers, the rock was wet, and my hands were damp, and the indentation where I was perched was slanted. Slowly I was sliding toward the edge of the cliff. I was trying to hold on to the rock but it wasn't working— there was nothing I could do. As my shoes slipped over the edge of the cliff, I remember saying in a trembling voice:

"Shit! Bruce, I'm sliding, what should I do?"

Sticking out of the rock a few feet to my right were thick tree roots, and in a last desperate effort I jumped toward them, grasping for something solid to hold on to.

I missed by only a couple of inches and plunged into the void.

In the end, Bruce was able to make his way back down without my help. When I woke up, he was kneeling in front of me, crying from joy because I wasn't dead. I'd fucked myself up pretty badly, though, with a cracked jaw, the skin on my knee and my hip ripped to the bone, and holes just about everywhere in my body. After landing on rocks then trees then rocks again, I had fallen over a hundred feet—the equivalent of eight stories. I sat up, my face covered in blood, and told Bruce in French:

"Don't cry, try to sleep," before promptly passing out again. Seeing that my back wasn't broken, he lifted me onto his shoulders and carried me down to our van. It took several hours and it was nighttime when we finally got there, completely unaware that forty-five forest rangers were searching the woods for us, because someone far away had seen me fall and called for help. I was bleeding pretty badly and was still unconscious. Bruce had been ripping up his shirt to make tourniquets, and when we stopped at the first restaurant on the road, he was wearing only his collar, perfectly buttoned up as always. Somebody called an ambulance while a girl claiming to be a nurse came to the van to see what she could do. Unfortunately, she passed out too.

When I woke up at the hospital the next day, I couldn't remember a thing. We stuck around for a few days while I convalesced and then we hit the road again. In our van, the Stones cranked up all the way, me with bandages everywhere and smoking joints between the metal wires holding my teeth together, we laughed our asses off 'cause we'd taken off without paying.

We got back on our way to California, going south this time: Massachusetts, Connecticut, New York. *New York!* Wow! We came down through Harlem at night. It had just rained and the sidewalks glowed under the street-lights. I'd never seen anything like it in my life. *Everything* was broken: shattered glass everywhere, turned-over trash cans, skeletons of abandoned cars, and especially graffiti—tons of it, covering more graffiti, which covered even more of it. As we passed in front of the build-ings, we could see it was the same story inside. This graffiti was made up of "tags," signatures and logos from each kid trying to identify himself in this urban wasteland. Each tag systematically indicated the name and street number of the artist—never anything else. It wasn't "Joe loves Mary," or "Free our nation," it was "Dog 132," "Killer 156," "Apache 149." There were also initials to mark each gang's territory, such as DTKLAMF, which meant "Down to Kill Like a Mother Fucker."

It was very hot. Everybody was on the street, standing in groups on and around each stoop. They wore white tank tops with tennis shoes or tight Bermuda shorts with white socks pulled up knee high, under which you could make out their packs of Kool Menthol cigarettes. Most of the women were enormous, their hair in huge Afros with white plastic combs stuck into them. Most guys wore do-rags, women's stockings they wore on their heads to flatten down their hair. Amazing!

From inside the van, I felt like everyone was looking me right in the eyes. I discreetly locked the door. . . .

We stopped near Columbus Circle, where a friend of Bruce's put us up for the night. When we came out the next morning, we found that our van had been vandalized. A window was broken and, worst of all, our cassette player had been stolen. Welcome to New York. Now get the fuck outta here!

We continued our journey: Pennsylvania, Ohio, Michigan, where we made a quick stop in Ann Arbor, home of Iggy Pop and the Stooges and the fabulous MC5. I knew a girl in Ann Arbor: Susie Kaminsky. I'd met her the year before on the banks of the Seine, serving as her guide/French kisser during her week in Paris. She had written me from the States, and I still had her address.

Susie looked like a Robert Crumb drawing. She was as nice as one could possibly be, and I wasn't surprised that she welcomed us like kings, even when we arrived on her doorstep without any warning. Immediately she took me into her arms shouting, "Phiilllliiiiipppe!!"

We spent the next few days at Susie's place. She and six roommates shared one of those gorgeous, classical, two-story wooden houses typical of suburban Michigan, with a large fireplace and a porch facing the street. There was a huge American flag hanging on the living room wall and posters everywhere: Angela Davis, Lennon, Lenin, Karl Marx, the Marx Brothers. . . . Susie would change my bandages as her freak brothers—radical students from the town—rolled hash-oil joints while educating me on Mao, Nixon, Vietnam, and others.

After giving Susie a big kiss we got back on the road. We went west a little: Tennessee, Arkansas, Oklahoma— where we bought a new cassette player, completely sick of the radio—New Mexico, Arizona. While the scenery was becoming spectacular, the van was becoming something of a tea parlor on wheels. We transported dozens of hitchhikers, who paid us in gas, sandwiches, or pot. Once, an adorable little hippie girl was even glad to make love to me, bandaged as I was, while we were rolling down the highway. What a feeling, fucking while passing other cars.

Almost every night we found drive-ins on the side of the road. I had never been to a drive-in before, and it was fabulous to watch old horror movies under the stars. We would park the van backwards, open the back doors, and watch the movie lying down on the huge mattress that filled the back of our van. Smoking joints all the while. Since our budget was limited, we usually snuck through the back once the movie had already begun. We only got caught once.

To keep the van running, we siphoned gas from other cars, squatting on all fours behind some parked car at four in the morning, sucking on a plastic tube to get the gas to come up. We'd stick it in our tank as soon as it started flowing. I did swallow a few gulps of gasoline, which I didn't really mind except one time when I got too much of a mouthful, and I started puking all over the van a few minutes later.

We often ate at Howard Johnson's. Their billboards advertised *All You Can Eat Chicken*—thinking, of course, that no one would eat more than two or three servings. Naturally, we went in equipped with a plastic bag, and after finishing our first serving, we would start to discreetly slip everything straight into the bag and then order more. We would leave with about a month's worth of chicken for the price of one serving. One time, after five or six free servings, the bemused waitress asked: "You eat the bones too?"

We stopped at the Hog Farm, in New Mexico—a hippie commune notorious for having succeeded in getting an actual pig on the ballot for the national presidential election. We took mushrooms, psilocybin, ate peyote in the Arizona desert while gazing up at the Milky Way. We were as free as the wind in the desert night, and really getting our kicks.

At each stop, there always seemed to be at least one girl wearing plastic pearl necklaces and a whole bunch of scarves around her neck, ready to welcome us, to roll us joints, make us dinner, and . . .

The pill already existed but AIDS didn't yet. American girls were liberating themselves, and I was happy to help.

A young Native American girl from a reservation in New Mexico gave us a few dried-up plants. She told us it was *Datura stramonium*, also called Jimson weed, promising us a fantastic trip, a mystical experience.

A few days later, in a motel in Flagstaff, we made ourselves tea with the funny-looking spiked plant. The smell was unbearable. After drinking this disgusting elixir, our mouths were kind of dry, but that was it, and after about an hour without anything happening at all, we concluded these plants had no effect whatsoever.

Somebody knocked on the door. It was a girl in a white dress with completely white skin and hair too. An albino, but with piercing blue eyes. She was strange and beautiful and was holding a white rabbit. She stepped into the room and sat on my bed.

Meanwhile, Bruce really had to pee, but he claimed there was another girl, a black one this time, in the bathroom. I opened the bathroom door laughing, but there was indeed a big black woman sitting on the toilet, smiling at me.

"Oh, sorry, miss. If you could please hurry up, my friend needs to pee," I said politely, before closing the door. Now there was a dog with very wrinkled skin in the room. We had no idea where he had come from either.

I was trying to hold a fascinating conversation with the blue-eyed albino girl, but the other one was still refusing to come out of the bathroom and Bruce was gonna pee his pants.

Over twelve hours passed before we started to realize that these two girls, the dog, and everything else in there were only extremely realistic hallucinations we could both see, like ghosts.

I also discovered that I had completely taken apart the air conditioner, perfectly aligning every little screw and bolt on the carpet. I seemed to remember that I'd thought it was the entrance to another dimension, but I must have been wrong.

The next afternoon, we started to slowly come down and only then did we discover that our wallets were missing! Unlike everything else, that was real. Apparently the maid had helped herself when she saw us happily talking to the walls. Our eyes were so tired that our vision went blurry, and we decided to try to find some info about what we had taken before we went blind. We went to the university in Flagstaff. There was a nun sitting between us in the van. I don't know how Bruce could drive. Once at the university library, we noticed there were hideous bugs on the walls everywhere. We asked a few students how they could stand it. They seemed surprised.

Finally we found an encyclopedia in which, with the help of a magnifying glass, we could read:

DATURA STRAMONIUM: LETHAL POISON.

After a long sleep in the van, we got back on the road. Our next stop: Grand Canyon, the little town right on the edge of the Grand Canyon, where an envelope holding a chunk of hash was waiting for us at the post office. Bruce's friend had sent it from Amsterdam. Unfortunately, we didn't know that the narcs were waiting for us there too.

When we arrived at Grand Canyon, the post office was closed. So we went to visit the famed canyon, one of the seven wonders of the world, before going to the supermarket. Here Bruce was arrested for trying to steal a leather puncher, and he was sent to the station to spend the night.

From his cell he overheard one not-so-bright cop telling another: "What do you know? That's the guy the narcs are waiting for at the post office!"

The next morning, I went to visit him, and he whispered the news to me through the bars of his cell. As soon as I left the station, I reasoned that since he was locked up, the cops wouldn't be waiting for him at the post office, which meant I could make the stuff disappear and get it back later.

I told the little lady at the counter that I was Bruce, and she handed me the package without even asking for my ID. Almost assuredly, she'd been told that a young kid with long hair was going to come pick it up. I went straight to the Grand Canyon to hide it under a rock.

Of course, it was the stupidest thing I could have done. I blame the *Datura stramonium*. . . .

They let Bruce go and we left town in a hurry, but we didn't get very far before sirens started screaming and three police cars surrounded us.

We were thrown in the back of two cars. Bruce was taken directly to jail in Florence, but since I was only seventeen, I got sent to the juvenile detention center in Phoenix.

There I was grilled by the narcs.

"Your buddy claims that you did everything." An enormous cop dressed like a cowboy was trying to get me to crack.

"He's going home tonight," he went on, lighting his cigar. "But you, Mister French Connection, you'll get blamed for the whole thing. Unless you talk. Where's the stuff?"

He must have taken me for an asshole.

I was thrown into a disgusting concrete cell with neither a mattress nor a window, with an old stinking blanket and an unusable toilet as my only consolations. They left me isolated in there for days on end, without even soap or a toothbrush. Nothing. The only person I saw was a sullen guard who brought me a cold McDonald's hamburger and a glass of water at 6 a.m. every morning and the same thing again at 6 p.m. every night. What a feast. . . .

After a week in there, I turned eighteen and so I was transferred to the Federal Penitentiary in Florence where I met up with Bruce once more.

Our new residence was a large white room completely enclosed with white bars, about thirty beds in two parallel rows, three long tables with benches, a TV bolted to the ceiling, and a toilet seat with no walls around it. You had to go to the bathroom in front of everyone. Have you ever tried to wipe your ass in front of thirty people? To pee standing up was also impossible. Having thirty inmates staring at you would block the whole operation. I think they did it on purpose. You'd find yourself standing there like an idiot, putting your dick back in your pants without having done anything.

"I can't pee!" I told Bruce.

"Do it like everybody else. Sit down!"

Every day, an alarm woke us up at 5 a.m. Immediately, we had to get dressed and make our beds, and then stand at attention for a short inspection. Afterward, we were let out in the courtyard for half an hour, then stuck back in the cage for the rest of the day. There was absolutely nothing to do but watch TV, smoke cigarettes, and wait for our dinner, served through the bars. At 8:30 p.m., the lights went out and, though ultimately nobody bugged me, I didn't sleep a minute my entire stay there.

There was one aggressive creep who tried to start something with me.

He started with, "Wanna give me a blow job?"

I took advantage of being French and pretended I couldn't understand anything. "Job? I-not-have-job, I-do-not-work!"—my accent pushed to the limit. It confused him, and he went to bug somebody else.

This huge black guy kept complaining of a toothache. For at least three or four days, he kept demanding treatment before he completely lost it and grabbed a guard's tie through the bars. Just like me, he was shocked to discover that the guards' ties didn't actually go around their necks but were pinned to the collar of their shirts. Those bastards thought of everything! The poor guy found himself standing there with the cop's tie in his hand as the sirens went off and five burly guards, armed with nightsticks, charged in to get him. In the end, I don't think they took him to the dentist.

A young Mexican guy with a nasty scar across his forehead sat next to me and started chatting. We talked of this and that for a while, and then he told me, "Be careful what you say and to who. Some inmates are cops looking to get a confession out of you, without you even knowing who you're talking to. Also," he went on, "be aware of prison codes. If an inmate offers you presents, like cigarettes or an orange, it's to let you know that he wants to visit you in your bed later on. If you accept his presents, it means you've accepted his offer." He then asked me why I was there.

"Oh . . . it's for a little piece of hash, but I'm innocent, it's a mistake," I said, hoping he wasn't about to offer me a few cigarettes.

"You know," he then told me, "for such a small crime, you shouldn't have to be stuck in jail waiting for your trial date. It could be quite some time—a few months for sure. If a resident from Arizona signed a paper to say that he's putting you up and pays your bail, you don't need to be stuck here. You can be let out on your own recognizance."

"Really?" I was suddenly very interested.

"Listen," he said, "I have friends in Phoenix who may be able to put you up. A little French kid like you, locked up here with all these motherfuckers, it's ridiculous. Write down your name. I'm getting transferred out of here tomorrow to do ten years in Tucson. Friends of mine are coming to say goodbye. I'll ask them if they can do it."

That evening, he was taken somewhere else, and I never saw him again. It was a shame, and I wish I could have thanked him, because a week later I was called: "419031!" Then I was taken into a room where two bearded freaks with pretty hardcore looks greeted me.

"You must be the French kid Carlos told us about. We're here to free you, brother."

They'd already paid my bail.

I couldn't believe it. That young Mexican who was gonna do ten years in jail had indeed taken care of it, and his friends—who didn't know me at all—were willing to put me up.

You got to admit, you meet some wonderful people in the penitentiary.

Fully expecting to do at least five years in there, I had prayed to God, "If you get me out of this mess, I'll never smoke a joint again for the rest of my life."

And now, after signing a few papers, my clothes were handed back to me and I was climbing into a beat-up old black Cadillac. Immediately, someone passed me a huge joint. Through a cloud of white smoke, I could see the jail shrinking in the rearview mirror.

"Thanks, guys," I said. "Listen, I've got a friend who's stuck in there for the same crime. Could you free him too?"

So that's how Bruce and I ended up spending two months awaiting trial in a house with about a dozen activists/leftists/anarchists/pot dealers/car thieves, with knives and guns at the hip!

They were revolutionaries. Or at the very least, complete nutjobs.

They strongly suspected the FBI was watching them,

and they expected they'd all be arrested any day now, and when that happened they were going to fight, guns in hand.

There were at least ten pounds of pot in the fridge and three stolen cars in the backyard—not even mentioning about a dozen guns of all types: revolvers, rifles, etc. One of them even showed us a hand grenade. This was definitely more fun than jail! The best thing was that these tanned outlaws not only lodged us, fed us, and gave us all the grass we could smoke for free, but they also lent us an old white Coupe de Ville convertible (probably stolen too) in which we spent our afternoons off-roading in the Arizona desert. What a fucking gas, skidding around in clouds of dust. We took full advantage of our temporary freedom, as we waited to either be thrown back in jail or massacred in our sleep by the FBI.

The lawyer who was going to defend us got in touch, and we went to meet him to discuss our trial. He was a public defender—a lawyer appointed by the state for those who could not afford to hire their own. He seemed very young to me. He started by telling us this was his first trial.

Why us?! we wanted to know. Now it seemed like we really were screwed. . . .

Actually, this turned out to be a genuine boon. Since ours was this young lawyer's first trial, he wanted to win *at all costs* and hopefully launch his career. At the time, every lawyer in the United States was required to do one free case a year for broke losers like us, and if we'd been appointed a big pro, all busy with his career, he might not have had the time or the interest in bothering with us. But ours, on the contrary, had everything to gain from winning our case.

He spent weeks working nonstop, actually driving from Phoenix to the Grand Canyon—an eight-hour round trip—to interview witnesses! Once he'd completed his huge case file, he'd managed to turn everything around: the cops were the ones that should have been sent to jail for having tried, unscrupulously, to implicate two obviously innocent hippie kids (us) simply because we had long hair. Throwing a French boy my age in a federal penitentiary was a scandal! And where was the hashish they were talking about?

Finally, after two months of waiting with Charles Manson, Che Guevara, and co., the big day came. In the end, the judge didn't believe a word of our noble defender's story, but lacking proof and especially lacking hash, they weren't able to convict us. Verdict: Not Guilty.

We left Phoenix that very evening.

That hash might still be in the Grand Canyon.

Phil, Amsterdam, 1973

GOING MOBILE

Phoenix, January 1973

WE WENT STRAIGHT FROM PHOENIX TO Los Angeles
. . . by hitchhiking!

Since they couldn't lock us up, the cops had kept our
van as revenge. It would take several months before we'd
be able to get it back.

Now, not only did we have no van, but I had no visa either.
To make matters even worse, I was now more or less wanted
by the French police for failing to show up for my army obli-
gations, as the draft was still mandatory there back in '73. I
only found that out when I called my parents to let them
know that my trip to the States was going great! The cops
had shown up at my parents' house and even went 'round to
my grandparents to see if I was hiding out there. In other
words, I had to hurry back home to be a soldier or else I was
going to be thrown in jail again—a French one, this time.

I already had my return ticket and my flight was scheduled to leave from Kennedy Airport four days later, which
was probably the only reason why the Grand Canyon cops
hadn't deported me.

Los Angeles wasn't exactly in the right direction. On
top of that, we didn't actually know anyone in Los
Angeles, but since it had been our original destination
when we first set out on this trip—before we were so
rudely interrupted by the narcs—we decided we had to
go to the end, if only for the principle of the thing.

We got lucky and were quickly picked up by a trucker,
who took us the whole way—all the while, listening to
country music in the ultra-high cab of his magnificent
solid-chrome eighteen-wheeler. We got to Los Angeles in
the pouring rain, exhausted and soaked, but still happy
to have made it to the end of our journey—even if along
the way we had lost a few pounds, a few teeth, our wallets,
our hash, and our van. Now there was only one thing left
to do: turn around and head back the other way!

We hitchhiked from Los Angeles to New York in less
than three days, which must be some kind of record. We
slept in the moving cars, and as soon as we got dropped off,
we kept going, nonstop from one end of Route 66 to the
other. First we were picked up by some California hippies,
who gave us a paper bag full of pot for the rest of our trip
before dropping us off a few miles from Phoenix, Arizona.
There, we were picked up by a young couple in a camper,
who asked if we had a joint. We pulled out our new paper

bag and started rolling it up. They were going far, these two, all the way to Oklahoma—almost half our trip—but they wanted us to finish or dispose of our grass before crossing into Texas, where the laws were harsh. This meant we were trying to consume about thirty joints while crossing Arizona and New Mexico. They took on a few more hitch-hikers to help us out, but we still weren't able to smoke the whole bag, and finally we just had to throw the two or three joints we had left out the window as we came up on the big sign that read: WELCOME TO TEXAS, THE LONE STAR STATE.

They dropped us off in Oklahoma City, where we were taken on by two girls in a Corvette going much faster than the speed limit. They looked incredible, one with red hair teased way up in a beehive and ultra-severe looking rectan-gular glasses, and the other with greased-up shiny black hair, in a DA, or Duck's Ass, like Elvis. They must have been les-bians. The one who was driving had a tiger head tattooed on her shoulder. She also had a gun between her thighs. They took us to Tulsa, where we were picked up by a trucker who took us to Nashville, then by another to Baltimore, and finally by radical hippies on their way to protest against the inaugu-ration of Richard Nixon in Washington, DC, where we made a stop to participate in the riot, surrounded by a few thou-sand students. There, we found some other hairy leftists, who took us all the way to New York. They dropped us off in Manhattan, in front of Grand Central. We had just enough time to say goodbye on 42nd Street, smoking the last joint I had hidden in my sock, and I jumped in a cab to Kennedy

Airport. Destination: Paris, but my charter flight was going to leave me in Amsterdam, where I would catch a train. This was cheaper than a direct flight from New York to Paris.

When I arrived in Amsterdam, I went straight from the airport to the station to catch the next train to Paris, but it turned out I had two hours to wait. I decided to take a stroll.

Already familiar with the city, I nonchalantly made my way to Vondelpark, where I crossed paths with a very pretty girl holding a baby. She was dressed only in white, pink, and baby-blue see-through fabric, and she and the baby—the same golden star drawn around their left eyes. I smiled at her and she started to talk to me, first in Dutch, then in English. She invited me for a cup of tea on her boat.

I missed my train. I stayed there for three months.

Janna and her son, Para, lived in a white, pink, and baby-blue barge parked on Keizersgracht, one of the city's many canals. She was a passionate Brian Jones fan, and a few pictures of him decorated the inside of the boat. There was an old cast-iron wooden stove at one end, and on a platform, a large bed covered with white, pink, and baby-blue furs. Para was a year old; Janna was twenty. I was eighteen and supposed to be in the army, but Janna—who had now dyed my hair orange—was hard to leave.

Finally, after three months, I was impatient to see my family again and now an actual fugitive from the law, so I went back to France to surrender. After warm greetings from my whole family, I went to the army reserve—my only goal being to get back out of there as quickly as possible. What a drag.

By showing up late, I was *"apte d'office"* ("not to be let out"), and they were going to send me directly to a disciplinary camp in Germany—a boot camp for hoods who, like me, had the nerve to show up late. Worst of all, they were going to shave my hair, which they hadn't even done at the penitentiary. Tough.

I really had to get out of this mess. My only chance was to get discharged.

I considered two possibilities: either as a hunchback (since I didn't stand too straight in the first place, I could exaggerate things until I looked like Quasimodo picking daisies and hope they found me too messed up to go), or, if that didn't work I could try to convince the shrink that I was insane, but that was probably going to be harder to do. I told myself that it would be better to show up hunchbacked *and* crazy, so that I wouldn't have to switch from one to the other in front of everybody.

The hunchback idea didn't go over too well. The little corporal looked at my hump, then stuck his knee behind my back and his hands under my arms. Vigorously, he pulled my shoulders back, straightening me up completely.

"Ah, you look much better like that, kiddo," he said. "The army's gonna do you some good!"

Okay . . . plan two. I made sure to do things like constantly pulling on the sleeves of my sweater and walking backward with my head down whenever anyone approached me, and I stood alone in the middle of the courtyard in the pouring rain. They sent me to the shrink.

It was obvious he was gonna be harder to fool and that rolling on the floor or repeating "caca-peepee-caca-peepee" and drooling wasn't going to cut it. It had to be something a little bit more subtle. I decided to improvise on the theme of a messed-up suicidal moron completely obsessed with his mother.

"So," he asked me, "what's the matter, son?"

"It's my mother. She told me I shouldn't go to the army."

"Really, why?"

"She told me that the other boys were going to do the same things to me that they did in school."

"What did the boys do to you in school?"

"*Nothing*!" I snapped back, looking terrified, pulling on the sleeves of my sweater.

"What do you like to do in life?"

"Uhhmm . . . I did a drawing for my mother, uhhmm . . . a drawing of my mother, a drawing . . . of my mother, it's to put in her room. . . ." I said, still tugging on my sweater.

This went on for about half an hour before he got tired of me and my mother. "Listen, son, keep drawing your mother," he said. "The army is not really the right place for you." He hit my file with a rubber stamp: DISCHARGED.

I stayed in character, keeping myself from leaping out of my chair and giving myself away. I'd heard about the guy who pretended he was deaf, then stood up with a big smile when the doctor, who was standing behind him, told him he could go home. You had to be careful not to blow it all at the last minute. A friend even warned me that they would sometimes follow you out of the place to make sure you weren't about to meet up with your pals at the corner bar to celebrate and brag. Knowing this, I pulled on my sleeves and acted like a moron all the way home, just in case they were watching. But in my mind, I was *ecstatic*! I was free!

I could pursue my artist's life!

After the performance I gave the shrink, I should have won an Oscar. I imagined the host saying to the three thousand people in the room: ". . . and for his breathtaking impersonation of a moron obsessed with his mother, Philippe Marcade takes it all."

On the other hand, it was a bit of a hit to my ego that I could pass for an idiot so easily, but still. I came out of that mess pretty much unscathed, except for my sleeves, which were hanging down to my knees.

After spending a little time with my family, I went back to Amsterdam to see Janna and Para on their boat. She was glad to see me, because she was about to leave on a tour with the experimental theater troupe she belonged to, and badly needed a babysitter for Para. I was right on time. In the blink of an eye, I found myself holding Para and the keys to the barge. Janna would be gone for three months!

Those might have been the happiest three months of my life.

I had no experience whatsoever taking care of babies, but that didn't seem to bother him in the slightest. On the contrary, I made him laugh.

Janna was well-known in Amsterdam, and being Para's nanny opened a surprising number of doors.

At the Melkweg, we were welcomed like kings. We arrived every evening at around eight and were instantly served a fancy vegetarian dinner with orange juice and hot milk. Para was really cute and everyone adored him. Although most people were pretty cool, I never let them hold him. There was one time when a guy with crazy eyes tried to feed Para a sugar cube, and I had to snatch it from his mouth. You had to be quick. "Please don't give acid to the baby, sir. Thank you."

At night, it was insanely cold on the boat, and Para slept with me in the big bed covered with white, pink, and baby-blue furs.

Life was serene in Amsterdam, alone on the boat with the baby. That was about to change: Bruce was coming.

Always a few steps ahead of everyone else, Bruce was now *punk* when he burst onto the barge in 1973. He'd cut his hair short and spiked it, and was wearing a black leather jacket with a skinny tie and black sneakers. He stood out like a fish out of water in the white, pink, and baby-blue boat, and when Janna came back a few days later she immediately couldn't stand him. The fact that he knocked over a candle and nearly set the barge on fire didn't help much, of course. . . . Still, she dyed his hair orange too.

Bruce and I were getting a bit bored of the hippies of Amsterdam, so we started hanging out a lot in OZ Achterburgwal, the red-light district. Here we discovered a small bar patronized by a bunch of young Vietnamese kids, who were quite generous with their super-hash.

One night, while we were smoking one of the joints they passed us, we noticed a strange taste. They'd mixed heroin with the hash and tobacco.

I remember that we seemed to be wonderfully floating on our way home, as we ate our "tartar hamburgers met mayonnaise." We had no clue what a mess this shit was going to get us into in just a few years. As he walked onto the boat, Bruce threw up everywhere—raising his ratings with Janna.

After a month of constant hell-raising, realizing that Para and I were more appreciative of his tasteless jokes than Janna, Bruce made up his mind to return to Boston.

By now, half of her theater troupe had started regularly hanging out on the boat, which was way less cool than being alone with Para and Janna. Honestly, they were starting to get on my nerves with their white, pink, and baby-blue stuff anyway, so I went home to France. With the help of my parents, I was able to get another month-long visa, and I went back to the States to meet up with Bruce.

Thirty-five years later, I'm still living here.

Bruce, Amsterdam, 1973

I LOVE THAT DIRTY WATER

Boston, February 1974

IT TOOK ME A WHILE TO get to know all the friends of the three nuts Bruce was sharing an apartment with on St. Botolph Street, in the heart of Boston. One morning, not long after I moved in, I was walking down the hall to the toilet, when I came face to face with yet another person I hadn't met—a young black kid this time.

I shook his hand, saying, "Hi, I'm Philippe," before casually continuing on my way to the bathroom. I was in the middle of peeing when I heard Bruce scream, *"Motherfucker!"* Then came a whole lot of racket, as if there was a big fight going on in the hall. I ran out to see what was happening, and found Bruce, in his underwear, holding the kid by the throat and punching his lights out. I'd introduced myself to a burglar! No wonder he'd seemed surprised.

The kid had grabbed one of the two medieval swords that decorated the wall of the hallway, and after meeting me, walked into Bruce's room, where he'd started filling his pockets with the change left on the night table.

Seeing that Bruce was waking up, the burglar had pressed the tip of the sword against Bruce's throat, warning him not to move. He must not have known who he was fucking with. Bruce grabbed the blade— cutting himself in the process—then jumped on the guy and took over. You don't want to mess with those Italians from Boston, especially in the morning! The three roommates came running to the rescue and, holding the guy against the wall, they searched his pockets. Then they told him, "If we see you again, we'll kill you. Got it? Go on, get the hell outta here."

As they threw him out, Bruce laughed, "We should have called the cops" before walking into the living room where he discovered, a little late, that the TV was missing. The burglar must have already taken it, then snuck it down the stairs when they threw him out, like idiots, without checking the rest of the apartment first.

There was a little local band that was just starting out, and we liked to go see them. They were sort of a Stones copy, with the singer and the guitar player howling together in the same mic like replicas of Mick and Keith. They were funny, these guys: Aerosmith. But they had some really good songs and one that was especially great: "Dream On."

We often went to a little movie theater that showed underground films. One night, we saw a movie we thought was incredible: *The Harder They Come* with Jimmy Cliff. It told the story of a "rude-boy," a Jamaican hood, who became a hit singer on his island before the cops gunned him down. We'd already heard of Jamaica and these rastas who constantly smoked pot to "get closer to God," but we didn't yet know their music, reggae, and we became instant fans. So when we saw an ad in the paper for a reggae concert, of course we had to go.

Sitting down in this small club, we immediately noticed a faint smell of grass, which seemed to be coming from backstage and we decided to go see if we could have some too. We opened a door that said "staff only" and followed the smell to a small room where five or six Jamaican dudes with dreadlocks were smoking a huge spliff. It must have been the band. We casually sat down with them as if it was nothing and the one closest to me, skinnier and less hairy than the others, passed me the joint. He must have thought we worked there. We chatted and I remember they were all very cool. After a little while, we went back out to our seats, completely stoned. The concert was really great.

The band, which we'd never heard of, was called the Wailers, and it wasn't until a few years later, when he became a huge star, that we realized we had—incredible as it may seem—smoked a joint with Bob Marley without knowing who he was.

We also smoked one with Joe, one of Bruce's friends, and after dinner at his house, he offered us a few more to take home.

In bed the next morning, with nothing else to do that day, I decided to light up one of the joints he'd given us. I noticed a strange taste right off and, after a few puffs, I started feeling queasy. Suddenly, the head of Marilyn Monroe on the Warhol poster on my wall came within three inches of my face and said, "I'm dead and so are you!"

It couldn't have just been grass! Instantly I was nauseated and overcome by a serious urge to puke, but as I got up to run to the bathroom, I discovered that my legs had shrunk. I had become a midget! On the tips of my toes, I made it just to the edge of the toilet seat and puked for what seemed to be forever. What a nightmare.

Meanwhile, seeing the door of my room open and half a joint in the ashtray, Bruce lit it and went back to his room. Hahaha! I seem to remember it went even worse for him!

"Oh, it was Angel Dust or PCP," Joe told us later on the phone, laughing. "I should have warned you. Did you like it? It's actually a tranquilizer for horses and elephants, you know? Great, ain't it?!"

Quaaludes were also real popular then. And guaranteed trouble. In Boston they called them "panty droppers." Two of these and you'd have no idea where you'd wake up the next day. Or who you'd be with.

At one point, we bought a whole bunch and sold them to friends. The problem was that they were "bootleg" and had a time-release coating, so you had to crush them with a spoon and put the powder in a gelatin capsule so it would work quicker. We couldn't crush them as fast as we sold them, and we often ended up with a few colorful "customers" in the kitchen, fucked up out of their minds, trying to get crushed quaaludes into tiny capsules and falling on the floor. We'd constantly be begging them to just keep their hands off the turntable!

Nan Goldin and David Armstrong, Bruce's best friends, were dreaming of careers in art photography.

Nan was very funny and spent most of her time discreetly snapping photos of everyone, trying to capture scenes that were intimate and spontaneous. She would show us the prints and everyone would grab the ones they were in. Who could imagine that twenty years later, these very same pictures were gonna be world famous? Or that one of Bruce and me was going to be on display, in large scale, at the Whitney Museum in New York?

We were both invited to spend a weekend at Cookie Mueller's, a friend of John Waters. She was a really great girl who had a house in Provincetown, a little seaside village on Cape Cod, to the north of Boston. Bruce didn't really know how to get to Provincetown, and the trip took us longer than expected. When we arrived around three in the morning, we couldn't even find the house!

After some doing, we finally found the place, but when we knocked on the door, nobody answered. We figured Cookie must have been fast asleep, and seeing that the door was unlocked, we came to the conclusion she'd left it open for us. We tiptoed inside. We couldn't see a thing, but we didn't want to wake her up by turning on the lights. We managed to locate a pullout sofa by groping around in the dark, opened it up as quietly as we could, and went to sleep.

I woke up the next morning to a rifle barrel two inches from my nose. A *huge* rifle, like in a Bugs Bunny cartoon, with this little guy in his pajamas at the other end. We were in the wrong house!

"What the hell are you doing here?" he demanded, ready to blow my brains out.

"And who the hell are you?" his son asked, pointing a second rifle at Bruce.

Still lying down, arms in the air, we explained our mistake and told them the address we'd been looking for. They both started laughing and proceeded to cook breakfast. The man went to get dressed, still howling with laughter, and when he came back down a few minutes later we discovered that, to top it all off, we'd ended up in the house of the town sheriff!

"How do you like your eggs?" he asked, buttoning up his uniform.

After breakfast, he pointed us toward the right house, which was a bit further down the road, and told us goodbye, still laughing. Cops were nicer in Provincetown than in Phoenix.

We immediately fell in love with Provincetown, a place where there were only a few old fishermen of Portuguese descent and Caroline, a girl of about twenty with tattoos all over her face.

There were also Ohni and Benton, who had a little house right on the beach, and about a dozen other nuts who had come from Baltimore, including Divine and John Waters. John had just finished his first three films: *Mondo Trasho, Multiple Maniacs,* and the legendary *Pink Flamingos,* in which Cookie had a part. It was in Provincetown that I first saw a guy with blue hair. Sure, I'd had orange hair before, but I'd never seen blue.

We decided to rent a summerhouse with Nan and David.

Our house was on Commercial Street, right in front of the sea. Bruce and I worked odd jobs, like washing dishes in restaurants, to finance our share of the rent. Whenever we finished working, usually around midnight, there would inevitably be a party starting somewhere.

We really had a good time in Provincetown—like that day when the TV in the house we were renting started fucking up, and Bruce decided to go steal the antenna from the roof of the house next door. Of course, the neighbor in question was watching his own TV at the time, and seeing that it was suddenly going out of whack, the guy came out to take a look and instantly caught Bruce. He called the cops.

They came back a second time, when the owner of the house we were renting—while showing around a prospective renter—discovered all the beautiful classic movie posters that had disappeared from the town movie house: *Psycho, Vertigo, A Streetcar Named Desire, Gone with the Wind.* . . . We had to give them all back, but—as nice as always—the cops didn't arrest us. They just sighed as they left, "Try to cool it with all that nonsense, will you?"

I think they were more bemused by this bunch of oddballs than anything else.

I remember one Saturday night, around five in the morning, they were throwing everybody out after a particularly noisy party. One cop pointed to Bruce, saying to his partner, "Look at this one, I bet he doesn't even know what day it is!"

"Yes, I do," Bruce snapped back. "It's Tuesday!" He was stoned out of his skull.

I had a summer fling with Nan, who took pictures of everyone on the beach every day. I think she actually preferred hanging out with the girls, and Provincetown had no shortage of ultra-cool ones like Caroline, Cookie and her girlfriend Sharon, and many others.

I totally loved listening to all the old records Bruce had brought with us to Provincetown. A whole stack of old rock 'n' roll 45s that I hadn't heard before: Gene Vincent's "Woman Love" and "The Swag" by Link Wray, "Cherokee Dance" by Bob Landers with Willie Joe & His Unitar and "Lonesome Train" by the Johnny Burnette Trio. "Tequila" by the Champs, the Kingsmen's "Louie Louie," "Wooly Bully" by Sam the Sham & the Pharaohs, but especially "I Put A Spell On You" by Screamin' Jay Hawkins and "Sleep Walk" by Santo & Johnny, which I played nonstop. Bruce also turned me on to old country music like Hank Williams, Patsy Cline, Loretta Lynn, and Tammy Wynette. Bruce had inherited from his two older brothers a gold mine of rare singles, such as "Rainbow '65 Part 1 & 2" by Gene Chandler on Constellation and other marvels. This was becoming my passion. From the Coasters to the

Shangri-Las, I must have listened to those old American records thousands of times without getting tired of them. Songs like "I Just Want to Make Love to You" by Muddy Waters, "Temperature" by Little Walter, "I'm Shakin'" by Little Willie John and "Tornado" and "Susie Q" by Dale Hawkins. Rhythm and Blues, Rockabilly, Surf. . . . Dick Dale, the Ventures, the Trashmen. . . . Soul stuff like "Try Me" by James Brown. Wow! And the girl groups: the Ronettes, the Chiffons, all the old stuff from the fifties and early sixties. And listening to this incredible music on warm summer nights, on the porch of that old, very typically American house with its little hanging lights and Bruce's old Ford Impala convertible parked out front only accentuated the effect. Where better to appreciate Eddie Cochran's "Summertime Blues," "I'm Gonna Be a Wheel" by Fats Domino, or "Don't You Just Know It" by Huey Smith & the Clowns. . . .

Speaking of clowns, the New York Dolls, a new band that was starting to make a name for themselves, was coming to play in Boston. Like Aerosmith, they were very inspired by the Stones but in a "Glam" way—dressed more or less in drag, makeup, hair teased to the max. They played retro-type rock, actually doing a few old covers, like the Cadets' "Stranded in the Jungle" and the Shangri-Las' "Give Him a Great Big Kiss," with it's famous intro: "When I say I'm in love, you best believe I'm in love, L-U-V."

On stage, they had the reputation of really kicking ass. They were the hippest thing at the moment, so we went to see them, and it was completely worth it. It was definitely one of the best shows I'd ever been to.

Afterward, we were approached by Frenchie, a New York Dolls roadie, who was getting kids at the venue to come to a party at the band's hotel. That's where we met Johnny Thunders, the guitarist. We spent a few hours with Johnny shooting dice in the hotel corridor, except we were using those oversized pink foam dice, like people hang from their cars' rearview mirrors.

Johnny and his girlfriend Sable Starr were really funny. Completely in their own trip, they had a contagious "I don't give a fuck" attitude. Johnny, an Italian from Queens, instantly got along with Bruce. They immediately launched into a hilarious conversation about spaghetti and the "real" Italian tomato sauce. It was a scene worthy of a Scorsese mafia movie: "No, you have to let it simmer for at least three hours . . . " and "If your tomatoes aren't ripe enough, you're wasting your time."

It was really funny to listen to this degenerate-looking "rock star," dressed all in black leather, swapping spaghetti recipes with Bruce. They went on like this for the whole dice game, and in the end, since the New York Dolls were coming back in two weeks to play the Boston Armory—a huge place—Johnny got our phone number with the promise that he'd come try Bruce's "real" Italian tomato sauce.

Still, we were pretty damned surprised when he actually called us two weeks later to invite himself and Sable Starr over for the promised Italian dinner. But we were even more astonished when they showed up, he in black leather and platform boots and she in a silver minidress—dropped off by a chauffeur and a limousine. They loved Bruce's tomato sauce!

Now that Johnny and his muse had eaten dinner at our place, we thought of them as friends, and it cracked us up to see all those autograph-seeking fans getting told to fuck off, while we were instantly treated like family. It only goes to show how a good tomato sauce can change everything.

After the concert, Johnny invited us back to his hotel to smoke, and we left the theater with the band, which meant getting shoved into a limo swarmed by screaming fans. What was really funny was that their hotel was literally right across the street; the limo just had to make a U-turn to drop them off on the other side. Meanwhile, the same fans had already crossed the street to wait.

During this very short limo trip, I heard an unhappy Jerry Nolan, the drummer, grumble to the bassist,

Arthur Kane, "That was a very good version of 'Jet Boy' you were playing. Too bad the rest of us were playing 'Personality Crisis.'"

Johnny gave me his phone number in New York, telling me to ring him up if I was ever in town. Way cool.

By now, Bruce was working as a hotel bellboy, but as I had nothing to do, I decided to call Johnny to say hi. "Hey, Flipper! Why don't you come over?" he said.

I didn't hesitate for a second. Bruce decided to come along. We hitchhiked from Boston to New York, which took seven hours, and when we got there, Johnny opened the door, looking a bit surprised, and said "Flipper, Bruce, what took you guys so long?"

He'd thought we were in New York when I called, and had no idea we were going to hitchhike all the way from Boston. Not wanting to send us right back, Johnny and Sable invited us to stay with them for a few days.

There were guitars and rock-star clothes everywhere, empty champagne bottles in piles of silk scarves and satin shirts, a pink fur coat thrown over a Fender amp, a luxurious rock 'n' roll mess. What a dream. A real rock star, who liked real tomato sauce and treated us like real friends. It was an honor. Unfortunately, he also liked real heroin. As soon as we got there, he offered us a line, which we snorted through a twenty-dollar bill.

Lying on the floor, I felt like I was melting into the carpet, or that I was made of sand and slowly being blown away by the wind until I'd completely vanished. Before vanishing, I went to puke in the toilet.

The next day, Johnny took us to a New York Dolls rehearsal. That was so exciting! We were their only audience, sitting on a sofa, rolling joints. Rehearsal was held in a big white room with white neon lights . . . somewhere. I have no idea where. I hardly knew Manhattan at the time and had no sense of where anything was in the city. It could have been Midtown on the West Side, but I'm not positive. Anyway, I remember they sounded incredible. They would stop in the middle of songs, talk a bit, crack a few jokes, light a few joints, play a few more verses. I'd never seen anything so cool in my life. The volume was so fucking loud, it made the whole room shake. I was in awe.

As they were wrapping up, I had the chance to talk some more with the other band members. They remembered me from Boston. David Johansen greeted me with a loud "*Hey, Frenchie!*" followed by a loud whiskey-throat laugh and an exaggerated wink. Syl was especially cool and funny and always seemed to be dancing in place as he talked. He spoke French very well, too—much to my surprise.

Jerry just kind of snubbed me, at first. It would take some time before I could gain his trust and friendship. Arthur was really nice, though quiet. He would mumble little jokes every now and then, looking bemused, in his pink tutu and white platform boots.

They always dressed insanely onstage. Except those weren't "stage clothes"—they dressed weird all the time. These guys were for real and as rock 'n' roll as anyone could want. Most of all, they struck me as "street"—"New York Street"—and not pretentious at all, even though they were way ahead of everyone else at the time.

After the rehearsal, we all went to eat at some diner somewhere. I think it was the Empire Diner, all in shiny chrome. I thought I had died and gone to Heaven.

After four days and four nights of drugs and rock 'n' roll in New York, we went back to Boston, dazzled. Sable Starr paid for our train tickets.

Winter in Boston was bitterly cold and Bruce was volunteering with a group of good Samaritans, bringing food to lonely old men and women who were having a hard time getting to the store because of the snow. That's how he met Conny, a ninety-four-year-old man with no family left, who asked Bruce to bring some pot the next time he stopped by!

"The other young fellow who came to see me before would bring me a few joints for my rheumatism," he told Bruce. Intrigued, I went to see Conny too. Conny Old Man, as we called him, was born in

Boston in 1879 and had spent his entire life there. "There were only horses here when I was a young man," he told us sucking on the joint like a pro. Conny Old Man had only one tooth left in his mouth and one joy left in his life: smoking pot while recounting his faraway memories to whoever would listen. And, of course, we were more than glad to be of service.

It was so touching to see that old guy overcome with joy as he relived his first love. "She was so beautiful," he told us, his big blue eyes shining with tears. "It was the spring of 1896 and I was seventeen." He was extraordinary, and his stories and old photos were so completely fascinating that we went to his place every two or three days to share our pot and listen to more of his adventures. Nothing in the world could have made him happier, he said every time.

"But nothing could make *us* happier, Conny. Light this one, and tell us what it was like to see electric light for the first time!" We would laugh and he would go off again for hours at a time.

The last time we saw Conny Old Man, the doctor had just come by. Conny was afraid he was going to be taken into a hospice soon, and he didn't want to go. We lit up a joint to distract him and stayed a little later than usual that night. We laughed, we cried; we loved him so much. When we came back a few days later, he was gone. Workers were painting his empty apartment.

He was already dead when we finally located him at hospice, just a week later.

Meanwhile, our apartment on St. Botolph Street was improving. The living room, in tropical jungle style, was now completely filled with huge potted plants that we had "borrowed" from the front of three or four Boston hotels. This was another of Bruce's genius ideas; he'd just been fired from the hotel where he'd been working as a bellboy.

"Nobody's keeping an eye on plants that are too big and heavy to lift." He convinced us pretty easily, and so three of us had gone around town, barely able to carry our plunder to our van. It was even worse when we got back to our building because we lived on the fourth floor. . . .

Our apartment was great but the building itself was always disgusting. One time, Bruce came home yelling, "Fucking hell! Somebody took a shit in the hallway!"

"It must have been a dog," I told him.

"No, it was *definitely* a person!"

"How can you tell?"

"Dogs don't use paper!" he said.

Bruce and I decided to become blood brothers. We went up on our roof at sunset to perform this whole sacred ceremony. Pressing a large knife against the palm of my hand, I started to chicken out and asked Bruce if maybe we could get something a little smaller—like a razor blade or something. But even those were still too scary. . . . In the end, we each punctured a small hole in our thumb with a tack and even that was no piece of cake. . . .

We were not the only crazy ones in Boston. Most of our friends were a little "out there" too, like Peter who was dealing coke while preparing to become a priest in a monastery, or Brian who had, among other things, lived in India, studied at Harvard, fought in Vietnam, knew the Beatles personally, was a direct descendant of George Washington, and *only* spoke in lies. At the beginning of our acquaintance, we always fell for his bullshit, but once we began to cotton on, we started asking for dates. We amused ourselves by cornering him in his lies.

"But weren't you studying the pyramids in Egypt at the time?" we would ask completely casually, as he mired himself in a little deeper.

There was also Brent, a big depressed queen, who was so lonely that he would call us up every other day to ask if he could come clean our place, and in exchange he could hang out with us a bit. It was pathetic, but at least the apartment was really clean.

In 1974, the big gay liberation hadn't happened yet, in which homosexuals and heterosexuals were separated into two camps. Although this would soon change, at the time, everyone was still lumped in the same bag—gays, artists, bohemians, beatniks, drag queens, rockers, hippies, musicians, leftists, druggies, Hells Angels, and whatnot. We were all united by the label "rejects of society," and we were all part of the same marginalized group hated by every other "respectable citizen." We were "different." We were "freaks."

Once again finding myself without a visa, I had to go back to France to renew it. Besides, I was really starting to miss my family, and I was eager to spend some time with them.

So I took a plane to Paris. Here I reconnected with a few old friends, like Francoise and Bruno, who took me to the Olympia Theatre to see a British band called Dr. Feelgood.

That was a true revelation. Short hair, tight black suits, thin wrinkled ties. Dr. Feelgood played sped-up old American rhythm and blues. They were fantastic. In one show, they blew away every other group of the time. No half-hour drum solos there. Just rock—sharp and bluesy, like the Stones in '64 but even more stripped-down and intense. They'd removed everything that was long and boring—something rock 'n' roll in general was starting to badly need. The genre was up to here with Yes and Emerson, Lake & Palmer and King Crimson and all those other clowns with their three-act rock operas recounting the story of an elf living on a green planet in the shape of a mushroom or some other bullshit. The Feelgoods were just in time to save rock 'n' roll, and they were doing so with impressive energy. Not only were they absolutely brilliant, but to top it off they were funny too. What a slap in the face!

They came from Canvey Island, where they ruled over a whole bunch of bands in the same style, such as Eddie & the Hot Rods and others. They called it "Pub Rock," and they were opening the door for a whole generation of punk rockers.

Nan Goldin sent me a cassette on which she had recorded herself saying: "Philippe, come back to Boston. We all miss you so much. I'll marry you if it'll help you obtain a visa, and if you'd rather, we wouldn't even have to consummate the marriage . . . if you know what I mean. Ha ha ha!"

I went back to Boston without any problems. I met up with Bruce and the whole gang. They were all set to move the scene to New York, where things seemed to be starting to happen.

Ohni and Benton, our friends from Provincetown had a huge loft in Soho, where they sold antiques that they brought back from Nepal every two or three months; they were doing very well for themselves. They had money and knew everybody. They were native New Yorkers, and as they adored me and Bruce, they decided to throw us a big party. Its only purpose was to initiate us into the New York underground scene and to introduce us to everybody. The invitations called it "A party to welcome Philippe and Bruce to NYC."

We'd been their favorites from Boston for quite some time, and they probably figured our arrival in New York was as good an excuse as any to throw a bash.

What an honor! The whole New York underground was there—people like Robert Mapplethorpe and Donyale Luna, the towering black model and ex-girlfriend of Brian Jones. She kissed me on the forehead and told me in French, "You remind me a little of Brian." There must have been about a hundred people in this sumptuous loft filled with Nepalese art, and as I was there to meet all these intimidating legends, I decided to drink a little to loosen up.

I was on my second glass of punch, which was in a big crystal bowl on the bar, when Ohni walked up to me and said, "You like the electric punch?"

At that very moment, the entire loft exploded into pink and green bubbles. Shit! There was acid in the punch and I was tripping! Talk about being sociable. I stayed hidden in a dark corner, checking my watch every half hour to find that in actuality only a few minutes had passed. . . .

So I was tripping on acid, trying to avoid everybody Bruce and I were specifically there to meet, when around one in the morning, four skinny little guys—or rather, three skinny little guys and one tall one—walked in. They all wore Beatles '65 haircuts and matching black leather jackets, white sneakers, and ultra-tight jeans. They started setting up their equipment, a drum kit and two amps, in front of the loft's huge window.

Cool! It was a band! And they had such a great look. The guests gathered around, so I did too.

They were called the Ramones.

They started to play. They were both fabulous and hilarious. Each song was exactly the same as the one before and always started with the bass player yelling, "One, two, three, four!" Every number, delivered extremely fast, with roots in rock and bubble gum, was shorter than two minutes, stripped of all guitar solos, played full blast, and the only lyrics their respective titles repeated over and over: *"I don't wanna walk around with you, I don't wanna walk around with you,"* etc. Their music was even more stripped down than Dr. Feelgood's. What a great band! Especially in the middle of all those artsy fartsy and beautiful people with their long hair and silver boots. These guys were the next wave for sure, the most anti-hippie band I had ever seen, the future of American rock 'n' roll.

A few years later, having befriended Dee Dee Ramone, I told him that story, and he said, "Yeah, but you know, that party at Ohni's was our very first show, even before our first club gig. We didn't know how to play."

Fortunately for them—and us—they never learned!

A**FTER A LAST DELIRIOUS SUMMER IN** Provincetown, we moved from St. Botolph Street to New York.

Nan, Cookie, Sharon, and many others were headed there too. I had no idea what I was going to do once I got there, but that didn't matter to me at all!

And so in September 1975, I moved into the Chelsea Hotel on 23rd Street.

Phil and Nan Goldin, Boston, 1974

*Phil, Walter Lure, Octavio, and
Julie and Johnny Thunders, 1976*

VENUS OF AVENUE D

New York, September 1975

THE CHELSEA HOTEL WAS THE MOST legendary of the bohemian hotels in New York, boasting such notable former residents as: William Burroughs, Henry Miller, Tennessee Williams, Sarah Bernhardt, Henri Cartier-Bresson, Gregory Corso, Diego Rivera, Edith Piaf, Dennis Hopper, Jimi Hendrix, Janis Joplin, Joni Mitchell, Leonard Cohen, and all the Warhol gang, like Edie Sedgwick, Ultra Violet, and Viva—star of the film *Chelsea Girls* in 1969. And also none other than Dylan Thomas, plus that Bob guy who stole his name. . . .

And a few years after our stay, Nancy Spungen would die at the Chelsea.

The Chelsea was really pretty cheap for what we got. My room was old and kind of funky, but it was also large, with high ceilings and two windows facing 23rd Street, five stories below. The hotel hallway was lined with paintings and other artifacts left by the famous artists who had once lived there. It gave off this vibe that incredible things had happened within those walls. I really loved the huge white stone staircase and the atmosphere of the corridors. It was quite . . . magical.

I found a job right away, working part-time in a store that sold reproductions of famous paintings. It was on 7th Avenue. I hardly knew the neighborhood, so on my very first night, I decided to take a little stroll and have a look around.

I didn't have to go far before I heard what sounded like Bob Marley's "Small Axe" coming from a bar across 23rd Street. The bar was called Mother's.

I went to check it out and was surprised to discover that the band playing "Small Axe" so beautifully was a bunch of white guys. When they started to play "These Arms of Mine" by Otis Redding, my mouth dropped open. They were *really* good and they looked *very* cool. I took a seat at the front of the stage to listen; it wasn't hard, because there were only about ten people in the room. The singer sounded a bit like a cross between Ben E. King and Van Morrison. He played a leopard-skin-covered Fender Stratocaster. I asked the waiter for the band's name, and he consulted a paper. "Tonight it's . . . Mink DeVille," he said.

Mink DeVille—my new favorite band—had just ended their third song, an original number this time, called "Venus of Avenue D," when I heard somebody shout behind me, "Hey, Flipper! What the fuck you doing here?"

It was Johnny Thunders! He had just come in with Jerry Nolan, the drummer. Apparently, I'd stumbled into just the right place. They joined me, and we ordered beers. Johnny told me how they had both left the New York Dolls to start a new band with Richard Hell, the bass player from Television. They were calling themselves the Heartbreakers and were scheduled to play at this bar in a few days. It was really cool to see those two again, especially since we now felt like old friends.

Bruce, David, and a few other friends were also at the Chelsea and just starting to look for apartments.

A few days later, we went to Max's Kansas City on Park Avenue South for the first time. Formerly the hangout of the Andy Warhol crowd, it had recently been invaded by a whole bunch of small local bands, all more or less direct descendants of the Velvet Underground. These were musicians like Television, Patti Smith, and others. Some people were starting to call these bands "punk rock," but none of them were in quite the same style as any of the others and no one really knew *who* was punk, but in general it meant, "Not too pro," "Not too good and proud of it," or something like that.

At Max's, there was a bar on the ground floor and a second floor where the bands played. Everything was painted black. The second floor also had another bar with a few pinball machines and tables pushed against the windows overlooking Park Avenue. On the other side, there were long tables and the stage was all the way in the back. The first performance we saw at Max's was Neon Leon, a tall black kid with a pink wig; he copied the Dolls a little but wasn't particularly good.

After the show, Bruce and I walked up Park Avenue South to 23rd Street, then over to 7th Avenue, where we ran into Johnny and Jerry outside Mother's. They were going to Avenue D to buy some heroin. It was three in the morning, and it was starting to rain. We decided to go with them, for the fun of it. We drove to Avenue D in the pouring rain. Everything was completely destroyed, a total war zone. Johnny stopped in front of the ruins of an abandoned building. Jerry quickly ran over to it while we waited in the car. He came back a few minutes later and gave us a little smile, which we took as good news, when these two guys came out of the building next door and went up to him.

"What's he doing?" Johnny hissed, looking at Jerry and the two Puerto Rican guys chatting in the rain. Jerry turned slightly, and immediately we saw that one of them had a gun to his head. They were mugging him, taking the bags of heroin he had just bought. I thought maybe they were going to kill him, then us—the witnesses. But then, out of the blue, a third guy appeared. Shirtless and very skinny, he limped toward them with a crutch under his arm and started yelling in Spanish, *"Do you wanna fuck around with Magnum's customers?"* The two other guys instantly shoved everything back into Jerry's hands, and he ran for the car. That little weakling with the bad leg must have been some sort of security guard for the heroin dealers—who were very powerful in the neighborhood—and the two losers must have known they wouldn't live long if they got caught mugging a dealer's regulars as soon as they made the transaction.

The next evening, I went back to Mothers' where the Fast, very much inspired by the Who, were wrapping up their show. Another band with a really cute girl got onstage. They were called Blondie, and they weren't *quite* together, fucking up a bit every now and then. But their singer, Debbie Harry, was gorgeous and their songs, which were kind of pop, were good. Again, the room was practically empty. The next day, on the other hand, when I went to see the Heartbreakers, it was completely packed. This was Johnny and Jerry's new band with Richard Hell on bass. Still, it was strange to see Johnny there. It was just last year that I'd seen him playing in

Boston in front of thousands of people. But still, they were fantastic: *"Born to Lose," "You Gotta Lose," "Blank Generation," "Pirate Love"* . . . so many brilliant songs.

After the show, a girl approached me; she wasn't much of a looker but she was pretty funny. She jokingly made off with the scarf I was wearing—one of those long Indian scarves from Benares, like Keith Richards always sported. After a little while, I decided to go ask for it back.

"My name is Nancy," she said. "I live around the corner. Want to come over? I got a little bit of . . . you know, if you're in the mood."

Nancy Spungen was a "dancer" in Times Square, which meant she was a stripper, or maybe even occasionally pulled tricks. She talked like a damn truck driver, with a "fucking" between pretty much every word: "Fucking people fucking giving me fucking shit for fucking nothing. . . ." She lived on 23rd Street between 8th and 9th Avenues. She had a little basement apartment with two small windows high on the wall, right under the ceiling, peering out at the sidewalk.

As soon as we walked in, she took out one of those little cellophane bags that were starting to become familiar to me. "I only have half a bag left," she said, taking out a syringe. "It wouldn't be enough to feel anything if we snort it. We should shoot it," she said. She got a spoon from the sink and wiped it. Then she added, "I don't really know how to do it. I only did it once. Can you do it for me?"

It didn't look too hard. You searched for a vein, and you could see blood come up as soon as you found it. I'd watched Johnny do it. After having filled the syringe with heroin, she passed it to me, and deciding to give it a try, I stuck the needle in her arm, noticing that she had way more than just one track mark. As for me, I still didn't want to shoot it. It looked painful. I snorted the rest of the bag, which ended up being plenty for me, because I found myself in her bed, fucked up out of my brain. I was so stoned I couldn't tell you if we had sex or not.

Heroin was the drug of choice in New York in the winter of '75. Looking back, it's hard to believe how naïve we all were. We didn't realize the danger we were putting ourselves in, nor how many friends we were soon going to lose because of it. It was the drug of the intellectuals, the artists, the cool, and the hip. Somebody could have at least warned us of the fact: that you won't be able to stop and that you will die. End of story.

Everybody did it, but no one said, "Three years from now we'll all be dead." Unfortunately, this was going to be true for Nancy and her future boyfriend, Sid, but also, later on, for many of our friends: Johnny, Jerry, Mark, Ritchie, Leon, Tony, Billy, Alice, and so many others. And those who didn't die from overdosing died from AIDS: Cookie, Genaro, Michael, Chris, Kevin, Alan, Cathy, Patty . . . sadly, the list is endless. So many

fantastic people, all so innocent, all dead so young . . .
for nothing. What a shame.

I got fired from my job at the painting store for showing
up late and hungover one time too many. I met another
French kid at the Chelsea—Octavio—a very cool guy,
and we started hanging out.

Bruce and David found a great ground-floor apartment
on Elizabeth Street in the East Village, right around the
corner from the Bowery and CBGB. This was another
club where all the bands from Max's and Mother's were
starting to play and it was across the street from the loft
where Nan Goldin would soon be living.

The room at CBGB was long, narrow, and downright
disgusting. It reeked of piss, beer, and dog shit, which
wasn't surprising since the owner, Hilly Kristal, let his
two skinny Afghan dogs shit everywhere. . . .
    The "stage" was nothing more than a piece of plywood
held up by four piles of phone books, and you had to
walk across it to get to the bathroom, which was right
behind the stage. Outside wasn't much better, as CBGB
was right next to a homeless shelter—"The Palace Hotel."
There were always at least one or two drunken bums
passed out on the sidewalk. At first, CBGB was solely a
Hell's Angels hangout, featuring only country and
Western bands. The club's very name, CBGB and

OMFUG, stood for "Country, Blue Grass, Blues and Other Music For Uplifting Gormandizers." Hilly Kristal, a large bearded man who looked like a lumberjack, was a cool guy. He'd been a Hell's Angel *and* an opera singer! He must have hesitated when some of these weirdos— like the four nuts from Ohni's party—started coming around asking if they could play at his club. . . . But when he saw the number of kids these bands were already attracting, all willing to cough up a few bucks at the door, it probably got him thinking. CBGB became a punk club out of necessity, and the Hell's Angels stuck around.

The first time I went there was to see Mink DeVille. I remember as I was standing in front of the club a bum approached me, asking for some change. "Sorry, but I'm broke," I said.

"Oh, really? Well, why don't you get a job, you bum!" he snapped back.

Ha-ha! My first New York bum!

I immediately loved all of Mink DeVille's songs, like "Mixed Up, Shook Up Girl," "Spanish Stroll," "Cadillac Walk," and especially the beautiful "Venus of Avenue D": *There she goes, there she goes, in her high-heeled shoes and her silk stockings, and her dress is so . . . tight, it's all right.* I was introduced to their singer Willy DeVille, and we hit if off right away. He had incredible class, and his girlfriend, Toots, was hilarious. She had a completely retro, early sixties style, with her black hair teased way up in a beehive, fishnet stockings, and a patent leather raincoat with the belt cinched tight and the collar up like Ronnie Spector of the Ronettes. They were both very outwardly romantic. Willy would step down off the stage and get on his knees in front of her to sing his saddest love songs. The rest of the band was also very cool: Reuben, Manfred, and Uptown Louie. They played soul and R&B as good as it can be played. They could have been Booker T. and the M.G.'s. They had *the* sound. You couldn't get less punk than Mink DeVille, but like all the other more-or-less retro bands of Max's and CBGB's— Robert Gordon, the Cramps, the A-Bones, the Zantees, The Fleshtones, The Bloodless Pharaohs, or Buzz & the Flyers—they all were thrown in the same bag. Willy must have hated that, and probably couldn't stand bands like the Dead Boys, Sick Fucks, or the Stimulators. One night he actually climbed onstage at CBGB announcing, "Hi, we're Mink DeVille, the only band here that doesn't have a song called 'I Feel Lonely and Sadistic!'"

Benton, Ohni's friend, had a loft on the Bowery, which he used as an artist's studio. He was right across the street from Nan's and therefore around the corner from CBGB, and right near Arturo Vega's loft, where the Ramones had just moved in. It was also two stories above Blondie's place—the band I had seen at Mother's a few days earlier, with their cute singer, Debbie.

One day, as I was going up to see Benton, I ran into her on the stairs. She smiled at me and said, "Hey, weren't you at Mother's the other night?" She had so much charm and was so cool, and I instantly fell in love with her, on the stairs at her doorstep. She invited me in and introduced me to the other members of the band—most of them lived there. Chris, her boyfriend and the band's guitar player (*oh well!*), was also very cool. He was just lighting a joint when the drummer, Clem Burke, came in and said, "Did you see the dead guy downstairs? There's a dead bum right in front of the building!" Debbie told him there were always bums lying in front of the building; sure they were dead drunk but they weren't actually *dead!*

"Oh, yeah, this one is really dead. He's covered with snow and frozen solid like a piece of wood. I touched him with my foot," Clem said. One after another, they all went out to see and came back saying, "Wow, he *is* really dead!" Then they threw themselves back in front of the TV without giving the guy a second thought. I saw him too, when I left the building completely in love. . . .

Johnny wasn't with Sable Starr anymore. He was now with a tall pretty blond named Julie. They'd just had a kid and a second one was on the way. They lived on Horatio Street in a cool but very small basement apartment.

I was visiting one evening, when Johnny went to the bathroom to shoot up. Somehow, he made the mistake of thinking that the sink was a chair, so he sat on it. The whole thing broke down under his weight. As he fell to the floor, he was violently sprayed with scalding hot water, which burned his shoulder and his back. There was water everywhere and Johnny had bright red patches peeling off his back. To top it off, he lost all the dope he was cooking up. Lovely evening!

Three months after my arrival in New York, I was still at the Chelsea Hotel and I still didn't have a new job. So I was thrilled when Johnny asked me to work as a roadie for the Heartbreakers, and, even better, he invited me to move into their rehearsal space—a loft on Grand Street near Chinatown. It was great, because their equipment was permanently set up there and I could spend hours playing the drums.

My father had been a drummer when he was young, and when I was thirteen, he bought me an old drum kit at a Paris flea market and taught me how to play.

For me, everything had really begun when I was eleven, during my sister Caroline's thirteenth birthday party in our living room. One of her friends had brought over a 45 by the Animals. It was "See See Rider" and it grabbed me like nothing had before. I knew "No Milk Today" by Herman's Hermits and French records like "Piccolo, Saxo et Compagnie" but this was entirely different. This was . . . savage.

Then, somebody put on another record: "Aftermath" or more precisely "Goin' Home," and that was a total revelation. If "See See Rider" had seemed savage "Goin' Home" was the jungle itself. Hypnotic, staying on the same note endlessly, punctuated by little screams and moans, it was the Voodoo mass, the sacrifice of the sacred cow, the ritual of fire. I couldn't understand a word of English, but I was sure they were talking about sex. It seemed taboo, X-rated. For eleven minutes and thirty-five seconds, the sound of the harmonica and of the Vibro electric guitar grabbed me by the balls. Who was that? I had to know more.

I will never forget when I first saw the album's back cover. The Rolling Stones! Wow, look at those guys! *Extremely* long hair, tight pants, Clarks, defiant poses, Brian Jones sitting in front, grimacing, a cigarette in his hand, and a glass of wine at his feet. Holy cow! They were cooler than cool and seemed to be . . . dangerous!

After "Goin' Home" somebody put on "Lady Jane," a slow number, and one of my sister's girlfriends asked me to dance. She was much older than me—at least fourteen—and had *huge* tits. Pressed against her, I immediately got a hard-on. Shit! I thought she might realize and slap me in the face, so I pulled myself away from her for a second to "readjust," hoping it would be less obvious that way. She gave me a strange look. She must have wondered what the hell I was doing.

"Umm . . . my lighter was a little crooked in my pocket!" I improvised, before pressing myself right up against her again, very pleased with my presence of mind to have so quickly come up with such a perfect excuse that, to top it off, aged me a bit. Perfect. . . .

"Lady Jane" unfortunately reached the end, and she took out a pack of cigarettes from her pocket, stuck one between her lips, and said, "Can I have a light?"

" . . . "

After that night, I never listened to a single word at school. I was too busy drawing imaginary Stones record sleeves or electric guitars or drum kits on the corners of the pages of all my schoolbooks. Being French, I actually thought that "Aftermath" meant "after mathematics."

From the moment my dad bought me those drums, I threw myself completely into practicing, spending my weekends working at it. By the age of fifteen, I'd formed my first band with friends from school: Revolution Nine. We played "The Letter" by the Box Tops, "Baby Come Back" by the Equals, and other hits of the day.

So I had a little experience with the music industry. I'd played twice in public in Paris, and, during a summer vacation, had won second prize at an amateur night singing contest at the Casino des Sports of Les Sables d'Olonne in 1967, playing drums and singing "Gloria" by Them. Some career!

So it was great to start drumming again ten years later. I would put on records, the stereo plugged into the huge Heartbreakers PA, and play all day long on the legendary big pink New York Dolls kit, the one featured on the cover of *Too Much, Too Soon*.

One day, as I was coming out of the loft, I came face to face with Octavio, my French friend from the Chelsea Hotel. "Octavio! What are you doing here? You coming to see the Heartbreakers?"

"Phil! The Heartbreakers? No, I just moved in. I'm staying with a friend."

He had just moved into the loft next to mine! We'd kind of lost touch for a while, so this was a completely wonderful coincidence. Since Octavio played guitar, we often jammed together in the Heartbreakers' loft.

If I'm not mistaken, it was in that loft that the Heartbreakers were photographed by Roberta Bayley. They were wearing white shirts with blood dripping from their hearts, as if they'd been shot. That picture became their legendary poster. The "blood" was actually chocolate syrup.

That loft was great. There was only an oven, a shower, a bed, a TV, and the Heartbreakers, who passed by every now and then to play "Blank Generation" or "Chinese Rocks."

One night I was watching TV when Johnny, Jerry, and Walter walked in and sat on my bed—the only place to sit—to have a talk. Johnny was pretty agitated. He started with, "When Richard gets here, I'm gonna tell him that from now on I sing all the songs and *he* plays bass and that's that. I'm not in *his* fucking band. I pick the songs and I sing them. He can play his bass and shut the fuck up."

Richard Hell arrived at the loft soon after, and before anyone could say a word, he announced, "Listen, everybody. From now on I want to write and sing *all* the songs. It was the original idea. Johnny, you should sing a song or two every now and then, but you're the guitar player and I'm the singer!"

Talk about an awkward moment. . . .

The Heartbreakers hired Billy Rath to replace Richard on bass. Unlike Richard, Billy hardly said a word and definitely didn't want to sing. Billy was quite nice but also quite . . . quiet. It was impossible to have a conversation with him because he never said anything. As their roadie, I went with them on a trip to Boston. The band demanded to get back to New York the same night so they could immediately spend their pay on dope. As they were sleeping in the van, Billy, who was driving, finally spoke to me: "I'm out of speed and I haven't slept in two days. Talk to me or I'm *sure* to fall asleep."

Unfortunately, he didn't say another word after that. Since I didn't have a driver's license to take over for him, I found myself stuck having to give a five-hour-long monologue along the lines of, "So . . . you like playing bass? Umm . . . you play well . . . Ummmm . . . yes . . . so . . . ummmm . . . good show tonight. . . . Ummm . . . it's nice around here.

. . . Ummmm . . . you don't like to play bass? . . . Ummm . .
." Once in a while I would ask him "Are you sleeping right
now?" to which he would only reply "Umm-umm."

Walter Lure, their guitar player, was the complete
opposite. Very well read and educated, his favorite topic
was history. It was always fascinating to chat with him. He
could tell you the exact dates of every one of Napoleon's
battles. Shame he wasn't driving that night. Walter was
also an excellent guitarist, a little bit in the style of Mick
Taylor. As it so happens, Walter is the one who played the
few existing guitar solos on the Ramones albums.

Meanwhile, Babette—a French girl I knew from Amsterdam—had come to New York and moved in with me.

We went to Provincetown together, where the whole
gang was going back to spend the month of August.
Then the Heartbreakers got kicked out of their loft in
September, and Babette and I lost our home. So I found
us a little apartment on 7th Avenue in Chelsea, and as
soon as we could, we moved in.

It was around that time that Wayne County, the hilarious
drag-queen singer of the Electric Chairs, broke
Handsome Dick Manitoba's neck. Handsome Dick was in
the Dictators, a pretty macho band from the Bronx. It
happened at CBGB during an Electric Chairs show. He'd
been standing right in front of the stage, yelling, "*Queer!*

Queer!" until Wayne County, wearing a white dress and growing increasingly annoyed, finally yelled back, "*You wanna come up on stage and fight like a man?*" Handsome Dick didn't hesitate, and started forward, and Wayne County instantly hit him with the mic stand. He was rushed to the hospital. A mic stand is *very* heavy, and Wayne County had just missed Handsome Dick's head by a couple of inches, breaking his collarbone instead.

Handsome Dick sued. A benefit show was organized at the Manhattan Center—a big room on 34th Street— to help Wayne County pay for a lawyer. Johnny Thunders was invited to play. He got together a band just for the occasion, featuring Walter Lure on guitar, Octavio on bass, and me on drums. That night was to be my big New York stage debut.

Octavio and I often talked about starting a band together, but he managed to fuck up his knee pretty badly while playing basketball with Johnny on Horatio Street one night. After spending a whole summer with his leg in a cast, complications arose, and he had to go back to France.

Mother's on 23rd Street closed down shortly thereafter, leaving only the memories of the very beginnings of all those bands. Die young, stay pretty. . . .

I cut my hair real short in the bathroom one night. I thought it looked great, real Steve McQueen. . . .
Later that week, I went to Max's with Bruce and Jerry Nolan. The bar on the first floor was as crowded as the

subway at rush hour, and Jerry accidently brushed against a glass someone had left on the edge of a chair. It knocked over and spilled. This guy dressed in a tacky baby-blue suit—probably a Studio 54 reject, a Mafioso, or a coke dealer—grabbed Jerry by his collar and spit into his face, *"Hey! That was my whiskey, asshole!"* I'm sure that if the man had been polite about it, Jerry would have offered him a new drink right away—after all, he got drinks for free at Max's. But since the creep took the belligerent approach, Jerry decided to clock him in the face with one forceful punch, quickly followed by another, then a third, then a fourth. Left, right, left, right, *bam, bam, bam!* like a machine gun, until the guy fell to the floor, more or less knocked out.

Jerry was just turning back to us, giving us a little smile, as if to say that was that, when the other guy, still on all fours on the floor, grabbed the broken glass and violently drove it into Jerry's balls. I saw Jerry's expression morphing into something completely different, and it became immediately clear to me that something was very wrong. Jerry was starting to fall forward when Bruce grabbed him by the shoulders and sat him down on a chair. There was an impressive dark-red spot rapidly getting bigger on the crotch of Jerry's velvet pants, and when I looked lower, I saw that it was pouring onto his feet. Blood was literally squirting onto his boots—it was unbelievable. I had never seen anyone bleed like that. Bruce took him by the arms and I got his feet, and we carried him out of Max's as quickly as we could, pushing everybody out of our way and spilling several more glasses. There was no time to wait for an ambulance. We laid him down in the back of a cab parked out front and screamed to the driver, "*Bellevue Hospital!!*" Bruce jumped in the front seat, and the cab took off like a bat out of hell.

I stood on the curb in the rain, watching them disappear down the street, when I slowly looked around and saw all the blood on the sidewalk. There was so much of it in the entrance to Max's that the staff was already washing it away with buckets of water. The whole sidewalk in front of the club was red. When I tried to light a cigarette, I realized my hands were also covered in blood.

The news had spread to the second floor, but it had been badly distorted on the way up, because people were stumbling out onto the sidewalk, freaking out, and demanding, "Somebody killed Johnny?" "Oh, my God! Where did all that blood come from?" "Who shot Johnny?" In all the confusion, I noticed the asshole who did it casually leaving Max's as if nothing had happened, trying to take off discreetly, without getting noticed. He probably thought he'd get arrested or maybe lynched by Jerry's fans. I strode up to him and blocked his exit, pinning him against the wall.

"Wait a minute. You're not going anywhere—just hold on. Nobody's going to hurt you, but just don't move!" I said, terrified and hoping he couldn't see it too much. After all, this guy had just stabbed Jerry with a broken glass, and my balls were all the way up in my stomach. We calmly brought the guy back inside to be identified, but of course the cops were never called and he was able to go on back to Studio 54 in no time. He hadn't quite reached Jerry's balls, like we'd feared, but he'd struck an artery less than an inch from them, at the top of Jerry's right inner thigh. After a few days in the hospital, Jerry was back at Max's, although he couldn't play the drums for quite some time.

© PHOTO BY DAVID ARMSTRONG

Bruce and Johnny at Johnny and Julie's wedding, 1977

Phil, Jorge, Reedy, and Steve, 1976

BOOGIE CHILLEN

New York, April 1976

JOHNNY INTRODUCED ME TO STEVE SHEVLIN, one of his closest friends.

Steve had been a boxer for five years—three as an amateur and two as a professional. He'd actually been a Golden Glove Champion twice in a row. You would have never guessed it from looking at him. Tall and thin, he had tons of class. He was always dressed in tight sharkskin suits that he got custom-made from a Puerto Rican tailor on Avenue B, and he wore them with magenta shirts with high tab collars and four buttons on the cuffs. He looked right out of *West Side Story*, a real New York dandy circa 1958–1960. He was the only person more fully in that style than Willie DeVille. They didn't come cooler than Steve, and all the girls adored him.

I started hanging out at his place more and more. Steve had an impressive record collection, especially when it came to old rhythm and blues: T-Bone Walker and Wynonie Harris, stuff like that. He also had a drum kit and a bass amp. He'd spend his afternoons playing bass along to records, and before long, I was sitting at the drums, backing him up. Soon after, two friends of his—Reedy and Jorge—started coming by regularly, guitars in hand. Jorge came from Mexico, Reedy from Liverpool. There weren't two of us from the same country; we were very international!

The four of us formed a band, and thus The Senders were born.

Soon we were playing every day at Steve's, and Johnny would often drop by to join in and smoke a joint. We were there practically every night listening to old R&B: a whole bunch of stuff like Bo Diddley, Howlin' Wolf, Muddy Waters, Elmore James, and especially Ike Turner's Kings of Rhythm, Slim Harpo, Little Walter. In other words, the Bible of Cool.

Reedy was incredibly funny, in a very British Monty Python kind of way. He was good friend with Max Blagg, and Max actually helped out with some great lyrics when we started trying to write songs.

Right away, we geared the band's sound and look toward old African-American rhythm and blues, menacing and aggressive. That style seemed way more punk rock than punk rock itself. On the one hand, we were inspired by sixties British bands like Them, the Rolling Stones, the Yardbirds, the Pretty Things, and the Animals, and the American bands from the same era like Mitch Ryder & the Detroit Wheels, Sam the Sham & the Pharaohs, the Mysterians, and the Sonics, and on the other hand, by all the rock 'n' roll and rockabilly from the fifties: Gene Vincent, Eddie Cochran, Johnny Burnette, Billy Lee Riley, Jerry Lee Lewis, Jackie Lee Cochran, Link Wray, Dale Hawkins, and all the others. But above all we loved all the black rock 'n' rollers like Little Richard, Chuck Berry, Fats Domino, Arthur Alexander, Rufus Thomas, Larry Williams, Andre Williams, Jackie Wilson, Screamin' Jay Hawkins, Percy Mayfield, Benny Spellman, Esquerita, Don and Dewey, the Coasters, Ernie K-Doe.

We all started dressing in clothes from Steve's tailor on Avenue B. Tight black suits, Puerto Rican magenta shirts with high collars and four buttons on the cuffs, thin ties, pointy shoes, greasy DAs. Like sophisticated rockers with a few broken teeth. Elegant dandies in slightly wrinkled suits quickly starting to look like a gang of insane Teddy boys who slept in their clothes. . . .

In October 1976, after a few months of rehearsals at Steve's, we made our big debut at Copperfield's, a club on 8th Street. Then the next day, we played at Max's. We played at two or three parties—one in the street in Soho, one in a loft in Chelsea—then at CBGB, Great Gildersleeves, then again at Max's.

Bruce, who was doing odd jobs here and there, decided to become our manager. But he found it too boring and quit after only six months.

We were scheduled to open for Blondie at the Elgin Theater, an old movie house on 8th Avenue. Arriving at the sound check, Debbie and Chris asked if I could help them with some French lyrics they were working on. "Oh, Philippe, we were looking for you," she said, beaming. We sat down in the middle of the room, and Debbie took a piece of paper out of her pocket and showed me. They were doing a cover of "Denise" by Randy & the Rainbows, but Debbie, being a girl and not wanting to appear to be a lesbian, had changed it to Denis.

Feeling that it sounded very French, they had decided to add a French verse or two to give the song a sort of "retro-French-Francoise-Hardy-beatnik-chic" feel. They needed my help, because I was probably the only French person that they knew in the scene.

She told me they were thinking of something along the line of, *"Denis, Denis, avec ton yeu est bleu?"*

"No, try . . . *avec TES yeux SI bleus*," I said.

"Okay, *si . . . bleus*. . . . How do I say 'I am crazy about you?'"

"*Je suis folle de toi.*"

"Um . . . no, it's too short."

"*Je suis SI folle de toi.*"

"Okay . . . a kiss?"

"*Un baiser.*"

"*Baisez-moi ce soir?* Kiss me tonight?"

"Hahaha! No, that would mean 'fuck me tonight,' Debbie! Try *EMBRASSE-MOI ce soir.*"

"Okay, it works: '*Denis, Denis, je suis si folle de toi. Denis, Denis, embrasse-moi ce soir, Denis, Denis, un grand baiser d'eternitee.*'"

In the end, "Denis" was an international hit, and I think it's fair to say that without my help it would have been a complete flop!!!!!!

After our set, we learned that Blondie had just canceled due to a money matter and things were badly degenerating in the room.

Since we were performing in a movie theater, the organizers of the event instead put on a movie about a British band we'd never heard of before: the Sex Pistols.

It was great. There was clearly a punk movement starting in England as well.

So the Heartbreakers went to England to join the Sex Pistols, the Clash, and all the others. They called it the Anarchy Tour. Before they left, they were developing a really cool look: sharkskin jackets, cuff links, black-and-white shoes, real New York rock 'n' roll chic. When they came back, on the other hand, they looked like clowns: big pink-and-green mohair sweaters and "bondage" pants with strips of fabric tying the legs together. They were completely "Sex Pistolified," which I thought was a shame. It was a little like they were now copying the band that had been copying *them*. Besides, I liked the new style much less than the old one. All these punks were starting to look pretty silly with their safety pins and their swastikas, and that style was becoming way too commercialized to still be cool. Everybody had a fake razor blade hanging around their neck now, and you could already find pink spandex T-shirts covered with zippers at Macy's. It was becoming a cliché. As soon as punk became acceptable, it wasn't punk anymore. How could you be rebellious and different if you were wearing the same uniform as everyone else? We, on the other hand, thought it was way more punk to dare to be something else. If you were punk, you weren't, and if you weren't, you were. . . .

It was complicated!!

After a show at Max's one night, we were asked to appear in the magazine *High Times*. We did a five-page spread in their fashion section, for their special punk edition, with Johnny Rotten on the cover. Although it would have given us a huge publicity boost, when we got to the photo shoot, we refused to put on the Day-Glo green crochet sweaters adorned with pink pom-poms, and the other crap they wanted us to wear. Our defiance both annoyed and amused the magazine guys, so they finally settled for having four punk girls surrounding us, striking different poses in various punk outfits, while we stayed as we were, in our shark-skin suits, looking like classic rockers. Haha! Pink pom-poms! Please . . .

That was around the time when I first saw the Cramps.

They played psychobilly! Ultra primitive rockabilly played by and for the insane. They had this way-cool girl guitar player, Poison Ivy, who didn't move an inch. Their other guitarist, Brian Gregory, was armed with a Flying V covered with black polka dots, and he spent most of his time onstage spitting lit cigarettes into the audience—his personal roadie immediately lighting another one each time.

The singer, Lux Interior, looked like Frankenstein witnessing a car accident. He stuck the *whole* microphone into his mouth—disturbing! They did great versions of "Domino,","Love Me," and other old unknown songs from the fifties, as if they had the same record collection as Bruce's brothers. After having played about ten such songs, the drummer, Miriam, got up in a fury, and told the band to go fuck themselves before attempting to storm off the stage. Lux blocked her way and told her to, "Play your fucking drums and shut the hell up!" She sat back down, still complaining, but started playing again. Everybody in the audience looked at each other in bemusement. The second time I saw them, the exact same scene occurred at exactly the same point in the show, and I realized it was part of their act and a complete setup. I laughed twice as hard that time!

I immediately fell in love with the Cramps and went to see them at least fifteen times over the next few years. I soon befriended them, especially Lux and Ivy, the politest, the strangest, and the most fantastic couple I've ever met.

Meanwhile, Nancy Spungen was growing more and more miserable because no one wanted to go out with her. She dreamed of dating a cool musician, like all her prettier friends were doing, but none of those guys gave a flying fuck about her.

She was the reject of a society made up of society's rejects. Not least, one must admit, because of the way she talked: "Fucking bastards only fucking interested in my fucking dope." To top if all off, by now, she was completely hooked on heroin. Nancy liked me and Babette a lot. It's true that we were probably nicer to her than most. One night she called me in tears to say, "I called to say goodbye, Philippe. I just slashed my wrists." She lived only a couple of blocks from us, so I ran to her place as fast as I could. Once I got there, completely out of breath, I found her with nothing more than a Band-Aid on her wrist. No blood. Nothing. I figured she must have been bullshitting me, and I asked her to show me what she had done. She refused. With that, feeling more and more sure like she was full of shit, I grabbed her arm and pulled off the Band-Aid. Holy shit! Not only there was a cut, but it looked serious, deep and wide. Ugh . . . horrible! I couldn't believe she could do that to herself. I tried to talk her into calling a cab to go to the hospital with me, but she didn't want to. Purely by luck, she had missed the artery and the bleeding had mostly stopped. I lit a joint to try to calm her down a bit, and she started to tell me why she wanted to die.

"None of those fucking bastards will go out with me," she said, sobbing. "Nobody can stand me . . . fucking assholes. Not a single one of those fucking guys will go out with me."

"None of them will go out with you 'cause you're a junkie, Nancy," I told her. "First, you'd have to stop taking that shit. You're a great girl, and you could very easily find yourself a boyfriend if you weren't a druggie. It *is* kind of repulsive, you know—especially for a girl. You need love, not heroin."

"*I need heroin!* I can't stop. Fucking shit, fucking motherfucking shit," she howled.

"You should leave New York for awhile. It's too easy and too tempting for you to get it here."

"Where would I go?"

"Anywhere, as long as it's far from your dealer. Go to France. Do you know Paris? It's beautiful."

"What the fuck am I gonna do in Paris? I don't even fucking speak French."

"How about England? They speak English in England. You should go to London. That's a cool place, London."

She calmed down a little and started thinking about it. After all, the Heartbreakers had just left for London, and she had a major crush on Jerry.

She could go over there, get rid of her terrible addiction, and become his girlfriend, in England. That was it, she had a plan.

I apologize to the Sex Pistols for having convinced Nancy Spungen to go to London. Maybe it wasn't such a great idea, after all.

So Nancy left her little basement apartment on 23rd Street and flew off to England. She called me before leaving to ask if I could take care of her records and her cat—a huge black cat she didn't know what to do with. Unfortunately, the cat was a junkie too! He was completely hooked on heroin—I'm not joking. Nancy told me she had left her dirty spoons in the sink too often, and the poor creature must have been attracted by the smell, or the taste, or something. It would go lick the spoons as soon as she was done with them. If heroin can hook a person so easily, it must have not taken much for a cat, and before long, he was desperately looking for dirty spoons everywhere.

We already had a cat, a very cute little black-and-white kitten named Poof. When Nancy dropped hers off, he didn't look too happy. He needed a fix, quickly, and was in no mood to play with Poof. That first night, he hid somewhere, but the next morning I was awoken by cat screams. I ran into the kitchen. Nancy's cat was holding a bleeding Poof by the throat and was about to finish him off. I grabbed the junkie cat by the back of his neck to restrain him—bad idea! He whirled around as if he was packed with dynamite, like the monster in *Alien*, and immediately plunged all his teeth and claws into my arm with incredible force. I almost passed out but instead started screaming. There were sixteen claws and I don't know how many teeth impaled deep into my forearm; he was gripping me extremely tight.

Unbelievable. I would never have imagined a cat could attack a person with so much violence, but a junkie cat . . . that's different.

He had been all right at Nancy's, but now he was going through withdrawal and was completely flipping out. I tried to pry him off my arm, but it was impossible—his hold was so strong, my arm would have been completely ripped to shreds. But I had to do something. The only thing I could think of was to knock him out—which I accomplished by hitting his head against the wall. I had to do it five or six times before it finally worked. He fell to the floor and I ran to the hospital. He got me pretty good, and thirty years later I still have the scars. It took a long time, and it was a sad sight to witness, but Nancy Spungen's cat finally managed to kick the habit. He grew into a good old cat, nice and all. Even his fur seemed to change and became full and shiny. As for me, I was all right. I needed a few stitches but I survived. Poof, too. We couldn't hold a grudge against him for too long, and in the end everyone got along fine.

Well, almost everyone. Babette and I were unfortunately getting along less and less and were using drugs more and more.

We were at Max's one spring night when, much too stoned, Babette suddenly got real nauseated and decided to step outside for some fresh air. There were always some disco lamos who came by Max's to check out that new thing they'd been hearing about: punk rock. One of them was just entering the club, wearing a white suit with his shirt open and a few gold chains around his neck. He looked straight out of *Saturday Night Fever*. He was starting to come up the stairs when Babette, standing at the top, right above him, suddenly threw up with surprising force, showering him with puke from head to toe. Uuurrgh! He stood there, completely shocked. It was running down his hair—he was covered in it.

"Oops, sorry!" Babette said with a little embarrassed smile. He was so shocked that he couldn't even answer. He slowly turned around without saying a word, walked back down the stairs, and went home. That was enough for him. At least, if he'd wanted to see punk rock, he got it!

That same evening, still at Max's, I met Phyllis, a very cute little brunette, and we chatted for some time. A few days later, I ran into her on the street, and she invited me to come up to her place. We started making out, but as I was still dating Babette, I was worried about getting caught. . . . I'd never done that before. So I decided to call home to see if Babette was there waiting for me, but when she didn't pick up, I concluded there was no rush and jumped into Phyllis's bed. After fucking for an hour or so, we got to talking and I told her how sick I was of Babette. Noticing the time, I decided to call home again to see if she'd come back or if we could hang out a bit more. I tried to dial the number but wasn't getting a dial tone. Suddenly, I had the troubling feeling that there was someone on the other end of the line.

"Are you having fun, Philippe?" asked a very familiar voice. It was Babette!!! Apparently I hadn't hung up the phone properly and it must have kept ringing. When Babette got home—probably only a couple minutes after I called—she picked up. She had been listening all this time . . . as if I had put a microphone next to the bed. Fuck!

At least, there was no reason for me to be nervous about getting caught anymore.

I went home to get my stuff.

Steve offered to put me up on 10th Street until I found somewhere else.

Steve's loft was great, but unfortunately, it was located between Avenues C and D, deep in the heart of Alphabet City. It was definitely a dangerous place to get to. You had to go through the jungle that started at Avenue A—dope house territory, no man's land. Between B and C, it got real cutthroat, and it was a terrifying place to venture into. Beyond Avenue D, forget about it—nobody ever came back from there alive! Once there, between 10th and 16th Streets, the scenery suddenly changed, becoming something of a huge esplanade where the New York Power Plant stood. This was the enormous complex that fed all of East Manhattan, the Lower East Side. Gigantic and majestic, it reminded me of the cover of that Pink Floyd record the name of which I forget. It was surreal . . . and imposing. That's where Steve lived. Well, not *in* the power plant, but right across the street, separated only by an old neighborhood swimming pool, which was all fucked up but still operating. To get to Steve's without getting a knife in your back, you were advised not to linger, to look like you knew where you were going, and to pray to God.

But the loft itself was great. Comfortable and spacious, with brick walls painted white. First there was the kitchen with a large wooden table surrounded by wicker chairs, then a main room with a sofa, an armchair, two Fender amps, a Ludwig drum kit, and two huge PA speakers—behind these a large punching bag hung from the ceiling. On the shelves against the walls, there were a few hundred records in alphabetical order, and a record player on the floor. Further into the apartment, there was more furniture, the dog bed belonging to Steve's dog, Jackson, and Steve's own bed. Then, finally, there were three large windows with a fantastic view. You'd think you were in Metropolis, with the power plant ahead, and to the right, at the end of the street, the East River.

The swimming pool right in front of the power plant was only frequented by Black and Puerto Rican kids, most of them no more than twelve or so; they were probably already dealers themselves and fearless. In the summer, they would all come back to the pool after closing time, climb the fence, and spend the night swimming and hanging out. The power plant behind looked like a relic of the nineteenth century and emitted a constant sinister hum punctuated from time to time by loud, mysterious, metallic sounds: "*crash*," "*vroom!*" It seemed to me the whole thing could blow up at any minute. And one night, that's exactly what happened.

It was July and hot as hell. I was in the loft chatting with Steve when the phone rang. It was Phyllis, the little brunette from Max's. She was screaming, "Philippe, I'm at home with Sable Starr, and we're terrified! The electricity went out. What do we do? It's pitch black!"

"Why are you calling me?" I asked, bewildered. "Don't you know how to change a fuse? It's easy . . ."

"No, you don't understand. It's not just us!"

"The whole building is out?"

"No, the whole avenue! We're looking out the window and we can't see anything. Help!"

"Wow, okay, don't worry. It's gonna come back on right away—they're taking care of it. Do you have candles? Call me back in ten minutes and let me know what's happening. . . . Don't be scared. It's nothing."

As soon as I hung up the phone, I told Steve what was going on. "Hey, they have no electricity on 6th Avenue. That was Phyllis. She's with Sable, and they're

flipping out because they're in the dark over there."
At that precise moment, the light bulb above us
started to flicker. We looked at each other, thinking
the same thing, and *wham*, lights out! Total darkness.
The TV stopped and we heard the powerhouse humming *much* louder than usual. Then there came
screams of terror from down on the street. We dashed
across the loft to see what was happening. After stumbling over the drum kit, I blindly groped my way
toward the windows when I heard Steve yell, "Phil,
look! It's unbelievable!"

New York City was in total darkness.

Lit only by the headlights of a parked car, you could
see all the kids running from the pool and clambering
over the fence as fast as they could, absolutely soaked.
Behind them, I could just make out the silhouette of
the power plant, like a gigantic medieval fortress, humming with rage. Suddenly, we heard a deafening *clontch*,
and the humming stopped. Now we were in total darkness *and* absolute silence. Soon we started hearing
screams in the distance, then police sirens blaring in
all directions.

It was the infamous 1977 blackout, during which
large portions of the Bronx and Harlem would be
torched and looted. It would also fill up every nursery
in the city precisely nine months later.

"Call Phyllis and Sable," Steve said, and we both
started laughing.

The telephone still worked, so I invited them over.

"You should be able to get a cab pretty easily on 6th Avenue. We'll get killed if we try to find one in the dark on Avenue D, and Steve is parked real far away. Let's face it, there are two Senders stuck here all alone in the dark!"

"Heehee! All right, we're gonna try. Make sure you hear the bell. Don't leave us stuck on the doorstep in the dark on Avenue D!"

"Okay, I'll tell Steve not to play the *electric* guitar and to turn down the TV! See you in a few." Steve found a little battery-operated radio somewhere, and we gathered around to listen. You'd think it was 1940. "*Things are already degenerating in the poorer parts of town. Army trucks are arriving in the Bronx and Harlem. The president has given the order to shoot looters on sight. Thousands of people are stuck in the subway where the heat is becoming dangerous. Firemen are trying to rescue the hundreds of people stuck in the elevators of buildings but are having a hard time moving around because no traffic lights are working and numerous car accidents are blocking every street. Only use your phone for emergencies, the lines are overloaded. Domino effect: the three New York power plants have broken down one after the other. Three cops killed. Stay home, do not go out, open your windows and take a quick cold shower if you get too hot, but do not waste water because of the fires everywhere. Six cops killed. . . .*"

"Hey, hasn't someone been banging on the door for a while now?" Steve asked suddenly.

I ran to the door, and immediately Sable screamed, "We've been ringing for an hour! You guys deaf or what? We were fucking terrified!"

"I guess the bell isn't working. Strange!"

From the window, we couldn't see anything but the headlights of cars passing by. It was like being in a forest on a moonless night. Little by little, candles started lighting up in windows, and the projects were glowing like it was Christmas. The next morning, we decided to take a walk to St. Mark's Place. The streets were one big party. Everybody was outside, gathered around restaurants and ice cream shops, which were handing out the entire contents of their refrigerators before everything melted or rotted. There were broken storefronts everywhere and other signs of the havoc from the night before. It was like we were in Beirut. Nobody had any idea when the electricity was going to come back on, and everyone was preparing for a second night in the dark. Some supermarkets were open—although without electricity—and people were lining up to get candles, flashlights, nonperishable food, etc. Cops were everywhere, and we saw a few army trucks headed toward Harlem, where the looters were apparently organizing for the night to come. Then, around 8 p.m., right after the sun went down, the electricity came back on, and as suddenly as it had started, the 1977 blackout came to an end.

Summers at CBGB, there were always as many people standing out front as there were inside the club. The sidewalk was where everything was happening. Inside, it was too loud and too hot, but in front of the club, you could breathe and chat and smoke a joint, which was prohibited inside.

One night, I was sitting on the hood of a parked car with Steve, Debbie, Jimmy Destri, Arturo, and Ty Stix listening to Dee Dee Ramone's hilarious rambling, when two Puerto Rican guys walked past, and one of them jeered, "Punk rock!"

"Fuck you!" Ty slung back, sounding jaded and bored. The guy immediately whirled around and punched him in the face. *Bam!* Then he just kept on walking as if nothing had happened, while Ty collapsed onto the sidewalk.

"You shouldn't have said anything!" Arturo said, as he helped Ty back up. We all started laughing, even Ty, though he was sporting quite the shiner.

Around two or three in the morning, the round trips back and forth between Max's and CBGB would begin. This was especially true for the girls, who would meet up with each other along the way, asking, "Have you seen Johnny? Is he at CB's?"

"No, they were all going back to Max's. Did you see them there?"

"No, we were just there. Television is playing. Who's playing at CB's?"

"The Dead Boys. We got sick of it. We're going to Max's."

They would meet at the same spot half an hour later and repeat the same conversation: "Have you seen Jerry? Is he at Max's? . . ."

There were always at least two or three of them dashing between Union Square and the Bowery, worried they were missing out on something. Around four or five in the morning, the action would mostly be in front of CBGB's, because there'd be the option of going to Arturo Vega's—the Ramones' residence around the corner—or to Blondie's loft a little further down, or Studio 10 right across the street. Or Bruce's on Elizabeth Street right around the other corner.

On my way home, around six in the morning, I would usually see one last girl somewhere on the Bowery, makeup running down her face, a glass of vodka in her hand and a cigarette between her lips, and she'd ask me, "Have you seen Dee Dee? Is CB's closed?"

Although most bands played in both clubs, there did seem to be two cliques: Max's bands and CBGB's bands. The Heartbreakers, the Fast, Wayne County, Robert Gordon, Suicide, Cherry Vanilla, the Blessed, the Cramps, and The Senders, to name a few, were Max's bands. On the other hand, the Ramones, the Dead Boys, Talking Heads, Television, Blondie, the Sick Fucks, and the Dictators were CB's bands. It mostly depended on where they had first started and where they played and hung out the most. For some bands it wasn't too clear, but for others, the connection was obvious. The Ramones, for example, were strictly CB's. I don't recall seeing them much at Max's.

Though only separated by a short distance, the two clubs were in completely different neighborhoods. CBGB was in the middle of nowhere, on the Bowery. It was Desolation Row, little broken-down buildings, vacant lots. Max's, on the other hand, was on Park Avenue South at Union Square, surrounded by huge and fancy buildings, most of which were office buildings or banks. Every afternoon, between 4 and 7 p.m., the ground floor at Max's was completely packed with businessmen in suits. It was happy hour, when people left work and came to drink and unwind a bit before going home to fight with their wives.

Drinks were half price during happy hour, and there were free hors d'oeuvres—mini hot dogs and tiny chicken wings in barbecue sauce—scattered around the room on hot plates. Happy hour was at the same time as sound check upstairs, so there would always be two or three punk rockers trying to make their way through the crowd of businessmen downstairs to catch the last of the free food. There were also the real desperate guys, like me, who would go to eat the free food even if they weren't playing at Max's that night. There were times when those mini hot dogs were all I survived on.

In front of CBGB, it was always the same twenty-four seven: drunk bums sleeping on the sidewalk and not much else. But in front of Max's, it was literally day and night. Since this was a business district, it was bustling with activity during the day—thousands of people in suits running in all directions—but at night, there wasn't a soul. *Nobody.* It was a ghost town, and the whole block belonged to us. Sometimes, we would pass each other, the businessmen and us, the punk rockers. Like vampires, we'd just be going home at dawn, as they were all arriving for work.

I loved the atmosphere outside Max's at night. It reminded me of a book from my childhood: *Tintin in America.* Nothing but big beautiful buildings from the thirties. No one there but us, drunk and stoned. It was easy to forget what that avenue was going to look like in just a few hours. Until sunrise, it was our private universe, our secret New York. When Park Avenue was Punk Avenue.

If you wanted to keep partying even after the sun came up, it was better to move to CBGB, where there were no offices to open, or executives to show up. Just the same old bums and Hell's Angels.

Late one night, I was smoking a cigarette in front of CBGB, chatting with Paul Zone, the singer of the Fast, when two huge Hell's Angels approached us. One of them, staring at my leather jacket, demanded of me, "Hey, you! You got a bike?"

Johnny had told me how a couple of Hell's Angels had once "confiscated" his motorcycle jacket for answering that same question in the negative. Apparently, they'd said, "Those leather jackets are for bikers *only*, faggot! Take it off or we'll beat the crap outta ya!"

"Too bad," he had sighed to me. "It was a real nice one."

With that in mind, I answered falteringly, "Um . . . yes."

The biker stepped closer. "Oh, really? What you got?"

He clearly didn't believe me, and I was starting to sweat. What the fuck had I gotten myself into? I thought I might have a better chance of getting through this if I dropped some unknown brand. I mean, I wasn't going to say I had a Harley. I thought back to my brother Eric—a "trial" expert—and his bikes, and I blurted out, "I have a Bultaco." I was shaking like a leaf.

"A *Bultaco*? Wow, great! Those Spanish dirt-bikes are the best in the world!"

Fuck! He knew his shit.

"What model you got? Where is it?" he asked, looking around.

"It's a 250 CC," I said, almost crying now. "It's in the garage, unfortunately."

This guy got right in my face, reeking of beer, and said, "You're cute," before heading into the bar with his friend, laughing all the while.

"Holy shit!" I gasped. Paul Zone seemed to think it was hilarious.

"He only spared you 'cause you had the balls to try and bluff him. You gained his respect with that move. Well, almost! A Bultaco, hahaha!"

Paul told me about a Hell's Angel at CBGB who would walk up to every girl he saw and say something to the effect of, "How are you, darling? Don't you remember me? I've been nuts about you for so long, you know? You're all I think of, baby, to the point that I've even got your name tattooed on my dick to prove it!"

The girl would of course protest, "You don't even know my name!"

"Are you kidding? You wanna bet? I'm willing to prove it to you right now, darling. You calling me a liar? We'll both go down to the men's room, and I'll show you my dick, and if your name isn't tattooed on it, I'll give you a hundred bucks. But if you lose the bet, you have to blow me, okay?"

Incredibly, a few of them actually went for it, convinced he was lying—or else they were very drunk. Possibly both. They'd find themselves stuck with him in the toilet, not knowing what to say when he pulled out his dick, on which was tattooed *Your Name* in blue lettering.

One of them, a bit more clever than the others, apparently told him, "All right, you lose. You said you had *my* name—not *your* name—tattooed! Hand over the hundred bucks."

We went to a party at Arturo Vega's and all the Ramones were there. At one point toward the end, when everybody was completely fucked up, I found myself right behind Dee Dee and Arturo, and I heard a little bit of their conversation.

"I've done everything. I've done every drug, every kind of sex, it's all become a bore. I've tried it all. What can I do now that I've never done before?" Dee Dee asked Arturo, who offered philosophically:

"You've never killed anybody!" There was a little pause, as if they were both contemplating, before Dee Dee said, satisfied, "Oh, yeah, I guess you're right!"

Hahaha!

The Ramones got along great with everybody, which was funny because they couldn't stand each other. They were at CBGB's all the time, and if they weren't there, they were probably around the corner at Arturo's. Johnny Ramone was always very calm, really nice, and very funny. He spoke in a nasally tone and had a strong Queens accent. All fast, short phrases. In a way, he was completely straight: a big sports fan, baseball card collector, the kind of guy who could tell you which team won what game at Shea Stadium in 1967. He was your typical All-American boy, a complete redneck with US Marines badges proudly displayed on the collar of his leather jacket, and he had a strong reputation for having right-wing political ideologies and for being a tyrant with the rest of the band. I'd been told he could be a real bastard and that he was hard to work with. Fortunately, I never had to work with him, so I only knew his good side; in my view, he was a very cynical guy, but he always had something funny to add. He was proud to say that he didn't think of a guitar as anything more than a piece of wood to slam three chords on, and he couldn't see any point in learning any more than that, or in having a "proper" guitar. "To do what?" he would reason. More than anything, he loved horror movies.

Joey Ramone was harder to get to know, because he was extremely shy. Tall and skinny, he would loom hunchbacked over you, give you a little wink from behind his thick glasses, and go on his way. It was two or three years before I finally got to have a normal conversation with him, and then I discovered he was a brilliant and extremely funny guy.

Tommy Ramone was even more shy than Joey. He had zits all over his face and never said much.

The one I knew best was Dee Dee. He was exactly like Dopey in *Snow White and the Seven Dwarfs* and was absolutely hilarious. Basically, he was the village idiot. He would look at you like a four-year-old who'd just got caught with his hand in the cookie jar. What a character. There was *always* a problem with Dee Dee, but never anything to be too concerned about. It was more like: "I don't know where my bass is!

How am I gonna play without a bass? How am I gonna play?"

"Dee Dee, your bass is right behind you, against the wall."

"*Aaah!* What's it doing there? Someone moved it? Who moved it?"

"You *just* put it there, Dee Dee."

"*Aaah!* You see, it's 'cause I take too many drugs. Why do I take so many drugs? I could take less! Why do I take so many?" He would give a long sigh and look at us with big googly eyes like a moron—always delighted to make me giggle. But behind this persona of a simple-minded oddball, Dee Dee was a true genius. He wrote practically all of their songs—words and music— all those classics that would define the genre, from "The Blitzkrieg Bop" to "53rd & 3rd." He'd even written "Chinese Rocks," the Heartbreakers' anthem, which he'd given to them after the Ramones rejected it because of its subject matter: heroin, Dee Dee's favorite drug.

Dee Dee liked me a lot. Especially, I think, because, like him, I grew up in Europe. He'd grown up in Germany, and it seemed to be an important and exclusive connection between the two of us. He liked to talk about it, "They can't understand, Phelllipp. They grew up in Forest Hills. Why did they grow up in Forest Hills? Where's my bass?!"

His girlfriend, Connie, was a nutjob. She was much taller than him and actually pretty dangerous. Their arguments were frequent and legendary. They had more than one boxing match on the sidewalk in front of CBGB. She was constantly confronting any girl she felt might be cruising Dee Dee, screaming, *"Who you looking at, cunt?!"*

It wasn't out of the norm to see Connie pulling a knife, or a pair of scissors, or a broken beer bottle, and we certainly saw Dee Dee running for his life out of CBGB a few times. But they loved each other so much and were so romantic together—for an hour or two.

Joey and Johnny weren't speaking to each other. Joey's girlfriend, Linda, had dumped him for Johnny, which caused chaos within the band. Besides, Joey and Johnny could not have been more different, with Johnny being extremely right wing and Joey your typical ultra-cool liberal New York Jew. Everybody wondered if they were finally going to shake hands or come to blows. In the end, they simply refused to speak a word to each other for twelve years.

As for Dee Dee, he quit the band, although he continued to write their songs from home, becoming something of the Brian Wilson of the Ramones.

In those days, everyone sort of laughed at the Ramones. No one thought of them as much more than a joke, a Mickey Mouse band—a great but limited concept, that would probably be forgotten long before the other bands of the time.

Just like Roosevelt and Kennedy, Joey Ramone now has a New York street named after him. Joey Ramone Place is on the Bowery, between CBGB and Arturo Vega's loft. There was an official ceremony with the Mayor of New York and everything.

Hahaha! He who laughs last. . . .

Nancy called me from London. She'd adopted a very pronounced Cockney accent.

"Hey, Philippe, it's Naaoooncy," she said all excited, as she started to tell me—speaking at a hundred miles an hour, with that incomprehensible fake accent— that she had finally found the boyfriend of her dreams: Sid Vicious.

"Sid who?" I said.

"Sid Fucking Vicious of the Sex Pistols!" she screamed. "I'm his girlfriend! I'm Sid Vicious's girlfriend."

It was nice to hear her so happy.

"Great, Nancy, the Sex Pistols. Wow! You see, life is great!"

So Nancy had caught a much bigger fish in London than Jerry Nolan. None other than Sid Vicious: El Sid, superstar of the day, the James Dean of Punk. The Sex Pistols were number one in England. The prettiest London punkettes would have given anything to be with him, but in the end, it was Nancy Spungen, our lame duck, who had won him over. Hahaha!

The Senders were playing at Max's on August 16, 1977—the night of Elvis Presley's death. Nobody gave a fuck, really, since he'd been "dead" since 1959. After his legendary records with Sun, he had served in the army in Germany, then came back and devolved into a fat and sweaty redneck performing in Las Vegas. But still, he was the King, and we played "I Feel So Bad" in his honor.

From August 18–20, we opened for the Heartbreakers at the Village Gate, a pretty big room on Bleecker Street. From behind my drums, I'd sing the Coasters' "I'm a Hog for You" and two or three other songs. We were starting to get noticed. After playing about a dozen shows as the drummer, the rest of the band decided I'd make a better front man. So over the course of one day, I was fired as the drummer and rehired, and we hired a kid named Billy Rogers to fill in on drums.

We played that way for the first time at CBGB. It was frightening—I had never really planned on being a front man, and I wouldn't be able to hide behind my drums anymore. But as it turned out, I immediately loved singing. I had an all right voice and I felt so much joy in putting it to use. I was in my element. Now I knew what I wanted to be . . . when I grew up.

The Senders were now a team of five, though we would have to go through a few drummers before finding the right one.

Speaking of drummers, I was hanging out at Blondie's loft one night, when Clem Burke—their drummer—showed me a record he had brought back from England, where they'd just been on tour. It was *Malpractice* by Dr. Feelgood.

"The *best* band in England! They're great!" he enthused.

Immediately, we launched into rhapsodies about Dr. Feelgood. "That record is fantastic! Do you know *Down by the Jetty*, their first one? I saw them in Paris back in '74, and then my pal Octavio and I went to see them on Long Island. Not too many people know them here—now there's at least three of us! At the Long Island gig, they were on the same bill as Papa John whatever his name is, the guy from Hot Tuna—a band with guys from Jefferson Airplane. An old black guy who plays violin for a bunch of hippies and Dr. Feelgood playing together. It was strange!"

"The Senders play 'I Can Tell.' Did you get that from this record?"

"Absolutely! It's funny because we played it with Johnny Thunders, who changed it a little. We also changed it a little from Dr. Feelgood's version, which is a bit different from the Pirates, which is itself different from Bo Diddley's original!"

"By the time it reaches Japan it'll be unrecognizable!"

"Dr. Feelgood came to play at the Palladium, opening for Gentle Giant—an even lamer hippie group than the other clowns from the Long Island gig — and they got booed off the stage. The Feelgoods actually got booed off the stage by the Gentle Giant fans, that night. I wasn't there—we were playing at CBGB that night. As it turned out, Dr. Feelgood actually came to see *us* at CB's. We were almost at the end of our show when Steve prodded me between songs, and asked, "Aren't those the guys from Dr. Feelgood?"

Indeed, I spotted Lee Brilleaux and the others right away.

"This one goes out to Dr. Feelgood!" I announced before launching into "I Can Tell," and to show them we were true fans, we followed with "Roxette," one of their songs we would often play for fun during rehearsal. I saw Lee Brilleaux saying something to Big Figure, their drummer. As they'd just been thrown off the stage by Gentle Giant's fans at the Palladium, he might have been saying something like: "I think we've finally found where the action is in this town. We should've played here!"

Afterward, he came backstage to introduce himself. I told him I would have loved to see them play at the Palladium and asked how it went.

"Um . . . all right," he said, then changed the subject. "Would you like a drink?"

Shortly thereafter, they came back to play New York again—this time at CBGB.

Johnny called me from London, where he was once again on tour with the Heartbreakers. "Hey, Flipper, it's Thunders, how ya doin'?"

"Hey, Johnny! What's new? Where are you?"

"I'm in London recording an album with a bunch of fags! Hey, you know what? Wilko Johnson has a new band called The Senders!"

"Yeah, right . . . and Lee Brilleaux's got one called the Heartbreakers, right?"

"No, I'm not joking. I just read something in New Musical Express. He just left Dr. Feelgood and started a new band called The Senders, I swear. He stole your name! Go lynch him!"

Johnny wasn't kidding, but he wasn't exactly right either. Wilko's new group was called the Solid Senders. . . . Not *quite* the same thing. There had been Roy Milton's Solid Senders in the fifties, an extraordinary rhythm and blues band, so the name probably came from that. On the other hand, he *did* see us play at CBGB—but maybe he didn't know our name. Or maybe he didn't like our version of "Roxette" and this was his revenge! Maybe we had a subconscious influence on him. He'd probably been stoned when he saw us, and later—although he couldn't remember where he'd heard it—the name Senders gave him a comforting feeling of well-being and serene joy. It's a theory!

It was too bad, though; we'd picked that name thinking it didn't mean much and no one would want to steal it. At first, we'd decided to call ourselves "Yakety Yak," from a Coasters' song, but before we even did our first show, we learned that was already taken. So, we figured a name like The Senders was a bit like the Ramones: most likely obscure enough that no one had thought of it. I came upon the name in the phone book; I was specifically looking for a band name, and the word "senders" caught my eye. There must have been about thirty Mr. Senders on that page. Joe Senders, Bob Senders. . . . Also, it was perfect, because the image was very rock 'n' roll. And also, though it wasn't much used much in the lingo of the seventies, "sender" often appeared in fifties rock 'n' roll songs, like Little Richard's "Slipping and Sliding." And, of course, you had Elvis Presley's "Return to Sender" and Sam Cooke's "You Send Me." A few people asked if we'd been inspired by William Burroughs's book *Naked Lunch,* in which he talked about a small sect of men who could manipulate other people's minds and called themselves "the senders." But none of us had read *Naked Lunch,* and we had no idea.

My mother had also discovered that there had been a little French band in the early sixties with that same name. She'd seen an ad in a collector's magazine that read, "Looking for Rare Vinyls, Very

Interested in 45 by the Senders," and she'd called the number. After some confusion, the potential buyer told my mother that the Senders cut their record in 1962—when I was eight!

So maybe I'd seen that record somewhere when I was a kid, and though I never knew why, that name gave *me* sort of a comforting feeling of well-being and serene joy!

Johnny called me a week later. He wasn't in England anymore but at Kennedy Airport, and he wanted to give me a souvenir from London. It was a pair of shoes. I don't know why he wanted to give me those shoes— maybe they didn't fit him. I doubt that before leaving London he thought to himself, *Oh, I think I'll go buy Flipper some shoes!* Still, it was very nice of him and those shoes were fucking great.

Two weeks later, he gave me a dog. He was on a roll! This was an adorable little black puppy he'd bought for Julie, but she didn't actually want it. I didn't know what to do with the puppy either, so I gave her to Bruce, who was thrilled. "Babe," as Johnny had named her, became the most important thing in Bruce's life. He would have lost his apartment, his car, and all his money before he let anything happen to Babe. She was sacred to him, and soon they were inseparable.

Once, Bruce drove our friend David to Los Angeles. He did NY to LA to NY round trip in only a week and, of course, he brought Babe with him for the ride. Trying to get to LA as quickly as possible, they decided they would never stop and would take turns driving so they could keep moving without losing any time. After driving for nearly twenty-four hours straight, Bruce figured it was his turn to rest a little. He said to David, "We've made great progress—we're really close. If we don't waste any time, we'll be in LA tomorrow. Your turn to drive."

They let Babe out to pee, and Bruce laid down on the backseat. David started the car and they hit the road. Three hours later, Bruce was comfortably snoring in the back and David was driving through the night listening to the radio. When Sonny and Cher's "I Got You Babe" came on, he started to sing along, "I got you Babe, I've got you Babe . . . Babe . . . Babe?!?! SHIT! BABE!!!"

Babe wasn't in the car. He'd driven off without her!

"My God, if Bruce wakes up, he'll kill me!" David told himself as he spun the car around, speeding back to where they'd last stopped, and praying that Babe would still be there. When he pulled up, three hours later, Babe was sitting right there, exactly where he'd left her. He slammed on the brakes, opened the door, and she sprang into the car, jumping on Bruce and licking his face.

"Babe, darling, Babe, stop it, calm down," he mumbled, waking up. He looked at his watch: "Fabulous! I slept six hours. We're rolling, rolling, we're gonna beat every record. Where are we?"

Bruce also had a pet monkey named Joseph. Joseph was a little squirrel monkey with a long tail and little round black eyes. He was the coolest. Bruce had bought him from a girl who'd kept him in a small cage since his birth, leaving him entirely crippled. At first, he couldn't do anything. Bruce put a few tree branches in the corner of his living room, and little by little, Joseph started climbing on them out of instinct. But he fell down every time. It took a while, but eventually he was able to climb perfectly, only slower than an average monkey of his kind. Though it's cruel to say, he became the perfect apartment monkey: wanting to play, but not too much; climbing, but at a slow pace. He would come hang out on your shoulder and check to see if you had a flea or two, then he'd slowly amble into the kitchen to get himself a banana.

During one of Bruce's many parties on Elizabeth Street, Andy Warhol came by with his entourage. As soon as he saw Joseph, he had to have him.

"Whose monkey is this? Darling, whose monkey is this? Oh, it's Bruce's? Where is Bruce? Darling, where is Bruce?"

He was introduced to Bruce.

"Bruce, this monkey is *fabulous*. I want to buy him. How much can I offer you for the monkey, Bruce *darling*!"

"Thank you very much, but Joseph's not for sale."

"No, *really*, I *must* have him. Darling, three thousand dollars? Five thousand? A painting?"

Bruce turned down every offer, but Warhol would just keep starting up again every ten minutes. "Ten thousand dollars?"

Bruce was pulling his hair out, but he just couldn't do it. He loved Joseph too much, and Andy Warhol never was able to buy him.

John Lurie and his little brother Evan were usual fixtures at the Elizabeth Street apartment. They would play endless games of *Monopoly* with Bruce, his girl-friend Mary, and Jim Jarmusch, while Babe and Joseph cuddled up and slept.

Mark Mahoney was often there too. He'd been a friend of David in Boston. Bruce lent him money to buy his first tattooing equipment. He would practice on oranges, and he offered free tattoos in exchange for the practice. Bruce got a couple that way.

Phil Marcade and Stiv Bators at CBGB's, June 1978

MY GAL IS RED HOT

New York, May 1978

1978 STARTED OUT WELL FOR The Senders. The audiences at Max's and CBGB loved us and things were starting to look up.

For Johnny Blitz, the Dead Boys drummer, however, things weren't going so well. He'd gotten stabbed on 2nd Avenue after looking for trouble with four Puerto Rican hoods, who didn't play around. He made the mistake of pulling a knife, which they ripped from his hands, and they stabbed him with it in his chest and throat. He barely made it out alive, and he left the hospital with more than 150 stitches. A perfect opportunity to celebrate! Hilly Kristal—who was now the Dead Boys' manager—decided to throw a benefit concert like no other. He organized a four-night punk festival at CBGB, and The Senders were invited to play. Also performing, among others, would be: the Ramones,

Blondie, Suicide, the Fleshtones, the Contortions, the Rudies, Helen Wheels, the Dictators, the Erasers, Corpse Grinders, Sick Fucks, Schrapnel, the Idols, the Criminals, and, of course, the Dead Boys, who had recruited John Belushi and Jerry Nolan on drums for the occasion.

From May 4–7, 1978, CBGB was overwhelmed by a huge crowd, forcing the bands to enter through a back door, which was a first. CBGB had never been so packed. There were just as many people out on the sidewalk as there were inside, because it was absolutely impossible to move around in the bar. We had the good fortune of going onstage on Saturday night between the Dictators and Blondie—a prime spot. I don't remember why we got to play at that time, since we weren't as well known as most of the other bands on the bill. Was it at Debbie's request? I can't recall, but I do remember playing our R&B in front of a wall of shirtless punks, out of their minds and drenched in sweat, jumping up and down in front of the stage, climbing all over each other trying to get fresh air to breathe. The energy and electricity in the air was ineffable. It was so crowded that we thought the room would explode. It was fantastic. After Blondie, the Dead Boys wrapped up the benefit and were besieged onstage by a gang of drag queens, including Divine, star of John Waters's films.

In June, we played at the Paradise Garage with Richard Hell and his new group, the Voidoids. The poster read: HELL IN PARADISE! Also on the bill were James Chance & the Contortions, Teenage Jesus & the Jerks, and the Stimulators. The Paradise Garage was a pretty big room on King Street, in the West Village, and normally functioned as a gay disco. It was completely packed—it was fabulous.

After the show, Debbie Harry took me aside to give me some advice.

"You should think about doing something on your own, Philippe. The band is great, but you're really special, you know? You could go far. Don't get stuck in the fifties retro trip. Think about the fact you could be very successful. Think of yourself first."

"Wow, thanks, Debbie! That's really nice of you. Do you really think so? But if I dumped the band I would have to find another one. I wouldn't want to play alone with an acoustic guitar. I'd probably find myself rehiring the band the next day!"

She laughed.

"You could actually make it. You don't realize . . ."

I'd just come off the stage; I was soaked and my ears were ringing. With the noise of all the people backstage and the racket the Voidoids were making onstage, I was having a harder and harder time understanding what she was saying, and she, therefore, was coming closer and closer to me and, when she was no more than an inch from my nose, I completely lost myself in her eyes. I didn't have *any* idea what she was talking about anymore; my heart was beating a hundred miles an hour, and I couldn't hear a thing—not even the crowd or the Voidoids. I was hearing violins and little birds, and had a strong desire to kiss her, but I held myself back. Then, in a blink of an eye, I came back to earth—all the sound returned, and I noticed she was looking at me, a little confused, as if she'd finished speaking and was waiting for an answer.

"Ummm . . . what?" I fumbled, mortified.

Toward the end of the evening, Richard Hell, James Chance, Steve, and I went to see the owner about getting paid.

"Come in, come in, close the door," this sordid character told us from behind his desk. Then he told us, "There was a problem, guys. Someone took off with all the money. Probably one of our employees. . . . I am furious and we're going to find out who did it. This has never happened before and I am so sorry."

There was a short silence, then Richard said, "You're joking, right?"

"No, no, it's true! All the money from the door was in a box that got stolen, everything! There's really nothing I can do, I'm sorry."

"Yeah, yeah. Just pay us what you owe us and cut the crap. I've got other things to do, okay?"

"I'm really sorry, guys."

That's when James Chance started to lose it. "Do you think we're just gonna say 'Oh, okay!' and leave? Give us our money, man. We don't give a *fuck* about your story!" He was screaming.

"I'm sorry."

"I don't give a damn that you're sorry! Where's my money, asshole?"

Steve elbowed me while looking discreetly behind us, and I noticed five huge bouncers had just walked into the room. They arranged themselves against the wall, arms crossed.

"Once more, I can't tell you how sorry I am. We're gonna see what we can do. Maybe someone will contact you later in the week."

I couldn't believe it, but the five big goofballs were actually getting closer and closer until they had us surrounded. One of them tapped me on the shoulder, growling, "I think it's time to go, okay? This way, please."

Someone told me that James Chance threw a trash can through the club's front window later that night. Right on, James!

Billy Rogers left The Senders abruptly when he won three hundred dollars in the lottery. He was replaced by a moron named Georgie. Georgie drove us to Boston when we took our first trip to play the Rat, a famous club. We got pulled over by the cops on a highway in New Jersey. The cop was polite and just told us that our bags were blocking the rearview window. As soon as we moved them, we could be on our way.

Immediately, Georgie demanded, "Show me your badge," and he took down the cop's number on a piece of paper. "My father is a lawyer. Do you want to know what happened to the last cop who tried to bug me?"

We couldn't believe he was doing this. There were three illegal aliens in the car and most of us were carrying pot. The cop had just told us we could go without any trouble. Georgie was out of his mind. We all sat still, silently gaping, when, of course, the cop replied, "Oh, really? All of you, get out of the car and show me your IDs."

He took our names and got back in his car. We were instructed to wait by the car. He was taking his time, and we were starting to get antsy, wondering what was going to happen. Suddenly two other cop cars arrived out of nowhere, and they all jumped on our guitarist Jorge, handcuffing him and throwing him into one of the cop cars.

Flabbergasted, we asked what was going on, and one of the cops said, "Your friend Jorge here is wanted in California."

Why?

MURDER!

How was that possible? Jorge had *killed* someone in California?

We had to call up the club in Boston to let them know we wouldn't be able to make it.

"Why?" they asked.

"Murder!!!"

It took a whole night before Jorge was finally cleared— the cops had got the wrong guy. But by then they'd also figured out that he didn't have a visa and wanted to deport him back to Mexico.

He was able to get out of it, but this whole incident had been such a drag that, fed up, he decided to quit the band. Eventually he went back to Mexico anyway.

What a blow! We had lost our main guitar player.

We fired Georgie immediately. And then, discouraged, Reedy decided to quit, too.

So, there was no one left but Steve and me. Things weren't looking too good for The Senders.

I got a job as a messenger in Midtown.

Meanwhile, Johnny Thunders got into an argument with the Heartbreakers and decided to do something else for a while. He called me from England and, learning of our situation, offered to join us for a handful of shows before we found a permanent guitarist. With that, he invited a young French guitar player named Henri Paul to join the party and soon they both arrived in New York. We recruited Ty Stix on drums. We did two or three rehearsals together at Steve's and were surprised when Johnny insisted on learning our songs rather than just playing the sorts of covers everyone would know, which would have been much easier for him. It was really cool of him to give us a hand in that way. With the publicity he was going to get us, finding a permanent guitar player would be easy. We booked three shows at Max's for August 3–5, then a fourth at Hurrah's. The ad read: *The Senders with Johnny Thunders.*

Those gigs at Max's were the coolest. The room was jam-packed, and with Johnny in the band, all the hippest girls in town now loved us all up!! Suddenly we were *the* band to see. By the fourth show at Hurrah's, it was total mayhem. In the middle of a crowd of over-excited degenerates, two girls started punching each other. One of them hit the other in the face with her stiletto heel, getting blood everywhere. The joint was jumping!

Our temporary lineup had a fabulous sound. It's a shame we didn't get to play longer with that group. After those shows with Johnny, The Senders became famous at Max's. Soon we found an extraordinary guitar player: Wild Bill Thompson. With his incredible power—already legendary on his native Long Island—he brought to the band his great bluesy sound and an ultra-cool presence, which accentuated The Senders' character even more.

On drums, we hired Tony Machine, who had replaced Jerry Nolan in the New York Dolls, before they'd finally broken up for good. With him and Wild Bill Thompson, the band reached a new level. It was thrilling to play with such strong musicians, though it didn't take me long to realize they were even crazier than Steve and I were.

Johnny made up with the Heartbreakers and Henri Paul had to go back to France.

I got fired from my messenger job.

About a week later, this girl Cathy—who I'd spoken with once or twice but didn't know well—came up to me at Max's and asked, "Is it true you're looking for an apartment? I'm leaving for Europe for a month or two, but I have three cats at home. If you'd like, you can stay at my place in exchange for taking care of them."

"Great!" I said, hoping her cats weren't like Nancy's junkie cat. But I didn't take her offer too seriously—she looked a bit nuts, and besides, she disappeared without giving me any more details. I figured she'd probably found someone she knew better to take care of them.

But then, passing by Max's a few days later, one of the waitresses came up to me and said, "Philippe, Cathy left you her keys and went to London."

"When?"

"The day before yesterday."

Shit, the cats! "Okay, I'll go there right away. Where does she live?"

"You don't have her address?" She was surprised.

It seemed nobody knew where this girl lived. I had her keys but not her address, and there were three cats rotting in her apartment. I got on the phone. I had to make a lot of phone calls and it took another full day before I got an answer, but I finally managed to find someone who knew where Cathy lived. And so in the end, I spent three months on 59th Street and 3rd Avenue in this beautiful little apartment. The cats had survived their ordeal, but unlike Nancy's cat, they held a grudge for quite some time.

After having squatted in Steve's loft for almost six months, I was happy to discover this new part of town. It was the exact opposite of Avenue D. It was luxurious, calm, and safe. I was two blocks from Bloomingdale's. It was a half-hour walk back from Max's, but I loved making that walk late at night. You went through Midtown, the business district, with all its towering sky-scrapers. I especially loved passing in front of the Chrysler Building—the most beautiful building in New York—and Grand Central Terminal, right across the street. Walking through Manhattan at night was often the best time to think up lyrics. A few Senders songs were written along those streets.

Cathy's place was great. It was a very cozy, very well-furnished one bedroom with a washing machine, a great stereo, and in the kitchen, about a hundred cans of Whiskers left for the cats. They were everywhere, that and dozens of cans of V8, the vegetable juice, with which she must have been dieting. I drank them all in a week. I was low on funds, and it was that or cat food!

All I had to do now was find a new girlfriend. I decided to go cruising. Arriving at Max's I immediately noticed a cute girl with black hair in a Cleopatra cut sitting alone at the bar. I decided to overcome my shyness and offer her a drink. I asked what her name was. "My name is W," she answered me, sounding annoyed. "W, W! It's like a double U. Like a double-you, W! Every word that starts with a W is like a double of you! All right? Doubles of you! Like 'wig'—it starts with a W and it's like a double of you, A-DOU-BLE-OF-YOU!!" She got a real scary look in her eyes and she tore off her wig, exposing a shaved skull. I ran to the other side of the bar. *Mommy!*

I started getting drunk. Johnny turned me on to a line of dope in the bathroom. Coming back into the bar, I noticed another girl who wasn't bad either. Maybe this one had real hair. I went to talk to her. I thought she must have been into me, because she started caressing my hand, but I was now completely fucked up. The whole room was spinning, and I didn't feel well . . . at all. I decided to step out for some fresh air. The girl came with me and we sat on the hood of a car in front of the club. Sweat was running down my face, and not even the cool fall breeze could ease the terrible nausea that heroin and alcohol can cause. If I had stayed still, it probably would have passed. But my brand-new girl-friend couldn't wait and made the huge mistake of trying to kiss me. When she suddenly started to French kiss me, I exploded, throwing up my whole dinner into her mouth. It was so embarrassing! She didn't take it well at all and left, showering me with insults. I, on the other hand, felt better now, but that was enough cruising for one night. I went home, walking in zigzags to 59th Street, ready to crash with three cats that hated my guts.

Eventually, Cathy came back from England with a British boyfriend, and I went back to Steve's, once again looking for a new pad.

I mentioned that to Willy DeVille, who immediately asked me to move in with him and Toots. It seemed like a perfect idea at first, but when I actually went to see the apartment I was shocked to find that they were both completely broke and deeply hooked. They had a German Shepherd that barked constantly, but there wasn't much else in that gloomy, messy apartment where a heavy junkie atmosphere reigned. Even though Willy was my musical idol, I decided not to move in with him. Not least because a really cool girl I knew, Maria, offered to sublet me her little flat on 17th Street, a hundred feet from Max's, for next to nothing while she went to Hollywood to launch a movie career. Maria's apartment was even better than Cathy's, and best of all, I could go to Max's in a T-shirt in January. Or in my pajamas. Or barefoot!

I was right around the corner from Max's, and the back of the club was directly across the street from where I lived: with the window open, I could hear the bands playing. When The Senders were playing at Max's, we used the apartment as our dressing room, as we could hear when the other band was done. It also made it much easier to invite a girl to my place, and soon, an adorable girl named Veronica moved in with me. We spent a few happy months together, but I fucked everything up and she left—although I don't remember exactly how. And then Maria came back from California and once again I was sent back to Steve's.

Then I went out with a really pretty girl named Debbie, but somehow I fucked that up, too. She later dated Paul Simonon of the Clash.

I slept around a bit here and there, but couldn't find a "keeper." One would think that since I sang in a known band at Max's, finding a girlfriend would be easy. The problem was that they were all more or less insane or else too fucking annoying.

Finally, I came across Risé, a great girl who I saw practically every night at Max's and to whom, as usual, I said hello.

"Yes, hello, hello, all right!" she answered me, sounding defiant. "How long do you plan on saying hello without doing anything else? If you don't take me home tonight, to hell with your hellos!"

So I married her.

We got married at city hall, both of us in white jeans, her

with her wild-child face and her big blond curls, Bruce
as our witness, David Armstrong as our photographer,
and no one else. I adored her, Risé. She was so tough.
She was my "Venus of Avenue D."

She was a tough cookie from Pitt Street. She'd been
one of the only white kids in her class at school. You
didn't step on her toes. She was a true New Yorker.

The night of our wedding, Bruce improvised a party
at his place on Elizabeth Street, and although we'd only
invited a handful of friends at the last minute, over a
hundred people showed up. They were in the apartment and on the sidewalk out front—most of them with
no idea who they were there for or why. Glen Buxton,
Alice Cooper's guitarist, must have known for sure,
though, because he brought me a present he'd made
himself: a little piece of cardboard he'd colored green,
with "Here is your green card!" written on it. You can
see that magnificent piece of art sticking out of my shirt
pocket in that great picture Nan Goldin took of Risé
and me at the party. It was later published in Nan's first
book, *The Ballad of Sexual Dependency.*

Risé and I lived on 6th Street at the corner of 2nd
Avenue, in a funky little place with roaches everywhere.
But we didn't care. We were happy.

With a loan from her dad, she opened a store on
7th Avenue at the corner of 10th Street. She called it
Rebop, and here we sold fifties-style rock 'n' roll

clothes: jeans, Cuban heels, pointy shoes, creepers, and retro paraphernalia like buttons and stickers. Risé used to work at the Late Show, a vintage clothing store on St. Mark's Place, and through her connections, she was able to get all kinds of used stuff for next to nothing, especially in Brooklyn. Motorcycle jackets by the pound, sharkskin suits in all colors, bowling shirts, pin ties, and black mohair coats. For the ladies: pedal pushers, those super-tight pants that stopped right below the knees, and sweaters, fishnet stockings, stiletto heels. . . .

We worked there every day with the help of our two employees, Billy Pidgeon and Michael-Gene, the guitar player for Buzz & the Flyers. This was the best rockabilly band of the moment, and Michael-Gene was probably the only guitar player in New York that could play as well as the incredible Cliff Gallup, from Gene Vincent's Blue Caps. He was *that* good.

Everyone was starting to get their clothing at Rebop, and for a while there, business was booming.

We would arrive every morning around eleven, tidy up a bit, and do a little vacuuming before opening up. One day, our vacuum cleaner broke down, and I had to take it to the repair shop. A few days later, as I was walking down 23rd Street to go pick it up, I passed in front of the Chelsea Hotel, and I ran right into Nancy Spungen. She had just gotten back from England.

"Philippe! How are you? I have to introduce you to Sid, he's right behind me. Sid! Come meet Philippe, my friend I told you about."

Sid Vicious casually strolled out of the Chelsea with his dog collar and his leather jacket. The perfect British punk rocker!

"Sid, this is Philippe," she said with her fake British accent. He gave me a little nod, hardly looking up, and looking like he really couldn't care less.

"That's so great! What are you doing here?" she asked me, all bubbly.

"Oh, nothing . . ." I said. "I'm on my way to pick up something. . . ."

At this, Sid suddenly became *much* more attentive.

"Oh, really? What you picking up?" he asked discreetly.

"Um . . . a vacuum cleaner," I mumbled, feeling pretty dumb.

"Oh yeah? A vacuum cleaner? What's that?" he asked, now *very* interested. I then realized that he thought it was New York slang for dope! Hahaha! A vacuum cleaner!

I started to explain: "A vacuum cleaner, you know . . . for cleaning the carpet. You plug it in the wall . . . it goes *eeeeeeehhhhhhh!*"

He looked at me like I was completely out of my mind. It was fucking great. There I was, actually trying to explain to Sid Vicious what a vacuum cleaner was!

Hahaha!

Steve, Johnny, and I were photographed in a restaurant for the fashion page of the *Village Voice*, the number-one weekly New York paper at the time. The photographer then took out a pad and pen and asked us where we'd bought our clothes. Even though it wasn't exactly true, Johnny surprised me by having the presence of mind to answer, "Rebop. Pants, shirt, Rebop. Even my socks!"

"And you?"

"Rebop. Shoes, everything, Rebop!"

"Me too," I said, winking at them.

The *Village Voice* was also the paper in which all our shows were advertised. The Senders took out the paper's very first color ad—black and magenta, of course—a quarter-page advertisement for a three-day weekend with the Contortions at CBGB.

There was also *Punk* magazine, a fanzine run by Legs McNeil and his pal John Holmstrom. Legs was really funny, and his magazine was pure genius.

But most of all, people read *Creem, New York Rocker,* and *Rock Scene,* a local magazine almost entirely dedicated to Max's and CBGB. Each page was covered with little black-and-white pictures of all the bands that performed at these venues. It was all pretty corny, with ridiculously bad little stories told in photo/comic-book style: "The Ramones take the subway," "Robert Gordon gets a haircut," "Blondie goes to the beach," "Cherry Vanilla goes to the supermarket," "David Johansen does some painting." Bob Gruen, a really great guy, took most of the photos. The Senders were in it quite a few times. I'm pretty sure the only people who bought *Rock Scene* were the people in it, but that was *everybody!*

We found an ad in there for a Long Island heavy metal band called Americazz, with a ridiculous photo of a bunch of hairy fatsos in spandex, trying to copy Kiss. Their respective names were under the picture: Keith, Davy, Alvin, JP, and Animal.

We were trying to decide which one was Animal and after a short debate, we all voted for the drummer—who was fatter and hairier than the others. The ad listed a phone number, so naturally we decided to call to verify.

Bill improvised, pretending he was a rock critic: "Yes, how are you? Bob Bijnveium, *Creem* magazine. I recently saw Americazz on stage and was extremely impressed. I would like to do an interview."

"Really?!"

"Yeah, yeah, it's a fantastic band, especially the drummer: Animal, he's unbelievable!"

"You mean JP? Animal's the guitar player. JP's the drummer!"

"Are you sure?!!"

"Well, yeah. I'm Davy, the bass player!"

"Ah! I thought Animal was the drummer. Oh well, never mind then, it doesn't matter, sorry. Have a nice evening!"

Calling Americazz became our hobby for a couple of months. We all did it one at a time, every two or three

days, with a new variation on the same scenario, and it
worked every time! As soon as Davy would say that
Animal was not the drummer, we'd cancel everything. I
claimed I was a journalist for the French music magazine *Rock and Folk*. Marc called himself the president of
Columbia. Davy must have killed himself—or switched
Animal to the drums!

One afternoon, I was walking up 2nd Avenue to meet
the band for a sound check at Max's, when I noticed a
dog tied to a tree. This wasn't too strange, but what was
unusual was that someone had left him a can of dog
food and a bowl of water. He was still there, tied to his
tree, when Risé and I came back after the show, around
five in the morning. I figured he must have been abandoned. We approached him slowly. He seemed well
behaved, a small German Shepherd or something sim-
ilar—a cool mutt. I got closer and reached my hand out
to pet him. He stood up, all happy, wagging his tail.

"Should we take him?" I asked her, immediately
seduced by his happy, smiling face. He seemed to be
saying, *Take me home! Come on!*

"He's cute," said Risé, like me crouched down on our
knees, petting him.

I untied his leash—an old rope—from the tree, and we
started to lead him down the street. He strolled between
us, staring up at our faces, looking absolutely delighted.
At home, he politely sat in a corner on the kitchen floor,

and we went to bed. The next morning, Risé went to the store, and I woke up to the dog licking my face.

"Oh, shit! There's no more coffee!" I told him, as I opened the kitchen cabinet. "I'm going to get you some food, and I'll bring back some coffee, too, okay, Doggie-dog? You stay right here. I'll be right back. We'll have breakfast together and then we'll go for walk. I'm going to buy you a brand new leash and dog shampoo, and tonight I'm going to give you a beauty bath. Cool, right? So don't move, all right? See you in a sec."

When I came back, only five minutes later, pot was scattered all over the floor. I ran to my desk, only to discover that the plastic bag in which I had left it was missing. I found it shredded to pieces on the other side of the room. There was nothing left in it. "*Fuck!*" I yelled, trying to gather all I could find while down on all fours. There wasn't much left. He must have eaten at least half of it, and I'd had enough for about twenty joints in there!

I told myself I shouldn't have left him alone in the apartment; it was my fault, and I would just have to train him. I found him in the kitchen, looking guilty. I had read somewhere that you can train a dog with a rolled-up magazine, so I grabbed an issue of *Rock Scene* from the kitchen table, rolled it up, and went over to him with an unhappy expression on my face. "Bad boy!" I said loudly. "Not good! You must not eat my pot—bad boy!"

Cornered against the wall, the dog got scared and he started to growl. Shit! It looked like I had a real problem now! He looked pissed—ready to bite me. I guessed that he was pretty stoned and the pot was making him paranoid. Or perhaps his previous owner had beaten him. I had no idea; I didn't know that damn dog at all! So I tried to defuse the situation, saying in a soft voice, "It's okay—good doggy dog. It doesn't matter."

GGGGGGGGGRRRRRRRRRRRR!!!

Fuck! Now he looked more and more like a fucking werewolf, with these diabolical red eyes and drool everywhere and teeth that were suddenly *huge*. Sure, I had some experience with junkie cats but none with pot-eating dogs. I had no idea what to do. Going really slow, I took two or three steps back and grabbed a broom. I put it between us to keep him off me. Using the broom, I guided him to the front door, as he continued growling more and more aggressively. Opening the door, I led him through the corridor to the elevator, then nudged him in it with the broom. I quickly pressed the ground-floor button as the door was closing, then ran down the stairs as fast as I could to show him the way out.

He took off running like a bat out of hell and disappeared down the street.

"Go, crazy dog, go! Good luck." At least he could have taken the food I'd just bought for him—in a doggy bag!

We had a show in Bethlehem, Pennsylvania. The crowd was especially rowdy that night, and the whole front of the stage, which was pretty high up, ended up collapsing under us, taking all of our equipment with it. We kept playing like that, on a slant, with our amps and cymbals on the floor, which almost caused a riot. We played every song we knew until the entire stage finally fell down.

After the show, we thought the owner was going to throw us out for breaking everything, but surprisingly, he was so knocked out by our performance that he immediately hired us back, promising us a sturdier stage.

That night, as we left the little town of Bethlehem at around five in the morning—wasted, of course—we were stopped at a red light when I noticed this white porcelain cat hanging on the wall of a pretty little house on the corner. Thinking it would make a nice present for Risé, I decided to go get it, asking the other guys to stay quiet and wait for me. I jumped the little picket fence, then tiptoed to the house and grabbed the cat, but it wouldn't come off. It must have been hooked on real good, and I was pulling on it as hard as I could, when suddenly Bruce started honking as all the other guys opened their windows and began shouting, *"Hey, mister! He's stealing your cat!" "Hey, wake up in there, goddamn it!"* and other stuff like that.

Another disaster was imminent, but I refused to give up and kept pulling on the porcelain cat until it finally came away . . . with a whole chunk of the wall! I sprinted back to the car with the guys still howling and honking, and just as I reached them, they took off, leaving me with nothing else to do but run after them, clutching a porcelain cat and a chunk of wall, hoping no one was going to open fire.

Johnny invited me and Risé to Thanksgiving at his mother's place.

He and Jerry picked us up, and we all left for Queens. Mama Thunders's house was typical of New York's Italian suburbs: thick carpeting, clear plastic covers on velvet sofas lined with little pom-poms all around. You could easily imagine Al Pacino coming out of the bathroom at any moment. I discreetly took a little peek at her bedroom and admired the ultra-kitsch ornate Roma furniture. My favorite part was the gold frame above the bed, which held a picture of Johnny onstage circa '73 or '74, with his skin-tight Frederick's of Hollywood Toreador stretch pants, tons of makeup and hair teased two feet high. Hahaha!

We ate in a basement that looked like it had once been a kids' playroom. At the bottom of the stairs, you were greeted by a painting of Johnny when he was about twelve or thirteen, dressed as an altar boy and reading the Bible. *The* album cover, I told myself! We all sat around a big table, with Johnny's statuesque sister, Marianne, and her tattooed husband, Rusty, as well as his mom and an uncle. There was so much food: a huge turkey, tons of stuffing, mountains of mashed potatoes, cranberry sauce forever! So delicious. His mom and sister were especially nice. They went to every

possible effort to make me and Risé comfortable.
Everybody was chatting and the atmosphere was jovial.
I was sitting next to Jerry, who kept nodding off. I figured maybe he had taken a bit too much dope before
coming; he looked like he could use a nap! More than
once, I had to discreetly pull him back up from falling
headfirst into his mashed potatoes. He would look at
me and say. "Eh?" before eating a little more and
starting to nod off again. Everyone was looking at him.
Oh no! After we finished eating, he fell asleep right
away in an armchair in the living room. Johnny found
an acoustic guitar somewhere and started playing a
new song he was very proud of: "You Can't Put Your
Arms Around a Memory." It was a gorgeous slow song,
with a hypnotic melody and the lyrics were absolutely
perfect. It blew me away.

I asked him, "Where did you get that phrase, 'You
can't put your arms around a memory'? I've never
heard that before—it's great!"

"I got that from *The Honeymooners*," he laughed. He
was talking about the fifties comedy series with Jackie
Gleason and Art Carney. I actually saw that episode a
few months later. In it, Ralph tells his wife Alice, "If you
don't give me the money I'm going to walk out this
door, and once I've walked out this door it's for good. I
will never set foot in this house again. You're gonna be
awful lonely all by yourself, Alice. And remember: You
can't put your arms around a memory."

To which she snaps right back to her fat husband: "I can't even put my arms around you, anyway!"

They still show reruns of *The Honeymooners* every now and then, and I saw that episode again last month. Although I'd seen it at least thirty times already, I still got goosebumps.

© ARCHIVES OF PHIL MARCADE

Risé, 1978

Steve, Phil, and Bill, 1979

RETURN TO SENDER

New York, October 1978

WE BECAME WELL ENOUGH KNOWN TO have a drink named after us at Max's. The ultimate honor! You could go to the bar and order a Heartbreaker, a Blondie, and now a Sender—which was vodka and I forget what else. If you wanted to die, you could always order a Suicide—an effective mixture of gin, whiskey, vodka, cognac, and anything else the bartender had on hand.

Once or twice a month, Max's would organize a jam night, where all the bands would get together onstage and play covers by a specific artist. Each jam night had a chosen theme. That night, it must have been the Rolling Stones or maybe Chuck Berry, and I went onstage to sing "Little Queenie" with Walter Lure and Lenny Kaye, after which Johnny joined them to sing "Too Much Junkie Business." With Jerry now on drums, the Heartbreakers were almost all onstage when James Chance, the Contortions' great little singer—and not one of Johnny's favorite people—climbed up. As always, he was perfectly dressed in his jazzy style, with an immaculate white shirt and thin black tie. He walked shyly up to the microphone and asked, "Do you wanna play 'Route 66'?"

Johnny was badly fucked up and replied, "That's right, go fuck yourself! No girls onstage, please! Come on, get off the stage, faggot!"

James looked bewildered and just stood there, not really knowing what to do. Johnny added, "Next! Yo, you can go home and suck your mother's dick!" Everybody in the audience laughed. No one was thinking this typical punk confrontation would go any further than that, when suddenly this guy no one knew—a real sleazy junkie in tennis shorts, with white socks pulled up to his knees—climbed onstage and jumped on James Chance, shouting, "You deaf or what? Move!" This guy punched James right in the face, a few times in a row. James Chance fell to the floor and that guy got off the stage to a hail of boos and whistles and was instantly thrown out by Max's bouncers.

James Chance slowly got back up, his face completely covered in blood, and he screamed into the microphone, "Do you wanna hear me sing fucking 'Route 66' or what?!" He was shaking like a leaf, blood pissing all over his white shirt. He started the first verse and the Heartbreakers continued to snub him, refusing to play a note. But they stayed onstage anyway, confused, letting him sing *all* of "Route 66" a cappella, to total silence. It was incredible. "Route 66" is a really long song, with I don't know how many verses, and he was bleeding profusely: from his forehead, his nose, his mouth. But he just kept going, without moving at all, until the very last note, when the room exploded. It was spectacular. I'd never witnessed such an ovation for anyone else at Max's, but he deserved it. What he did was downright extraordinary—a pure rock 'n' roll moment. The Heartbreakers didn't know where to throw themselves.

We put out our first record in the fall of '78. This was a 45 that we financed ourselves with the money we were starting to make. "The Living End" backed with "No More Foolin' Me"—two original numbers we'd recorded a few months earlier. We had a thousand pressed, which we sold quickly by mail—two dollars a record—with a little ad in *Trouser Press*, a national publication. We got orders from practically every state in America—except New York. We concluded that we were more loved in places we hadn't played yet!

One night, after a rehearsal in Steve's loft, we were hanging around the kitchen when someone—I can't recall who—called us on the phone.

"Quick, put the TV on!" they yelled. "Nancy is dead. They're talking about it."

We all ran to the TV and stared, open-mouthed, as the news anchors announced, "Punk-rock star arrested for the murder of his girlfriend." We saw the cops leading Sid Vicious out of the Chelsea Hotel—he was in a black suit and handcuffed behind his back. Then two paramedics dragged a body bag on a gurney. What had happened? She'd been stabbed?! *Found dead in the bathroom,* they were saying, *rolled up in a ball beneath the sink, a knife in her stomach, Sid in bed sleeping.* Each channel contradicted the other. Sid had confessed it all. . . . Sid swore he was innocent. . . .

We'll never know who killed Nancy, in the end. Maybe Sid did it. Maybe she did it herself. Sid could be violent, it's true. The last time I saw Nancy, she had a big red mark over half her face, and she told me Sid had thrown his burning-hot coffee at her. But she was capable of cutting herself, too, as I had witnessed before she went to England.

Of course, it could have been someone else altogether. But who? And why? And if it was Sid, what could have motivated him to do it? Nancy, on the other hand, could've easily had reasons to kill herself. Maybe things weren't going well between them. It seemed to me that if she thought she was going to lose Sid, she would *never* willingly go back to the way her life had been before. She would never let those other bitches—who had spat in her face for so long and who were now green with envy—have the pleasure of enjoying their "revenge." I knew she would rather die than let that happen.

No matter what actually happened, it was sad. Nancy was nice. I don't know . . . everybody put her down, but I thought she was nice. She was a little like the punk Cinderella, the one who never got invited to the ball, but who ended up with the prince. Would she have ever imagined that she would become such a legend of punk rock, with books still written about her thirty years later, her own biopic, and her name known the world over?

Nancy's mother wrote a book in which she claims her daughter gave away her cat and trusted me and Babette with her "treasured" record collection, but that she could never reclaim them because we "disappeared" shortly before she returned to New York.

I found that funny, because we never went anywhere, and with upcoming Senders gigs a constant feature in the *Village Voice*, it wouldn't have taken a rocket scientist to find me! But what I found most ironic was that I actually tried several times to give Nancy her records back, but she wouldn't even hear me out

"Hey, Nancy, want your records?"

"Shut up!" she'd give me a dirty look.

I would tease her about them, because they were mostly Rod Stewart albums and stuff like that and, of course, she didn't want Sid to see her with those. Haha! I remember a Cream album and Cat Stevens.

Those records ended up scattered here and there over the years. Babette may still have a few. I only have a copy of Traffic's *The Low Spark of High Heeled Boys* with a very girlish "Nancy Spungen" written on the back cover in light blue marker. There's also blood splattered on it, probably from when she shot up.

I don't know how I ended up in the subway at rush hour—probably I was headed to meet the others at a sound check at the Rocker Room uptown. But there I was, rolling toward 86th Street, crushed by a mob of New Yorkers leaving work, while I had only just woken up. When the door closed, this huge creep in a suit pressed against me, looked at me sideways, then elbowed me hard in the stomach. It hurt pretty bad. I was wondering if he'd done it on purpose, when—still staring at me with the same expression—he did it again. That time with full force. He then gave me a defiant look as if to say: *You wanna do something about it?* I guess he didn't like my look. It was the only thing I could think of, because I hadn't done anything to that idiot. I couldn't breathe, and he was starting to scare the shit out of me. He was this big, red, sweaty, macho asshole in a suit, who probably went to the gym every day with his stupid crew cut and his big aggressive shithead face. He must have had a bad day at the office. Maybe his secretary didn't want to blow him anymore. In the crowded subway, nobody saw anything, and even if they had, they would probably have turned away anyway. That guy was enormous and this was New York. I wanted to cry out for help but it would've have only pissed him off more. And besides, after they got a good look at me, the others which probably tell him to hit me harder! And then he'd invite them all to join in the fun! I could only hope that he wouldn't have time to kill me before we reached 86th Street—which fortunately was the next stop.

The train finally pulled into the station, and a mass of people spilled out, like ants when you step on their nest. The guy got off, too, and disappeared in the crowd. *Thank God!* I told myself, making sure to avoid him. Still a bit shaken, I lit myself a cigarette as soon as I passed the turnstile. I couldn't believe it, but when I got to the bottom of the stairs, the movement of the crowd forced me right behind the guy. Luckily, he didn't see me. He was carrying one of those attaché cases that are open on top, and there were a few papers sticking out. I couldn't help myself. As we reached the top of the stairs, I dropped my lit cigarette into his case and watched him go strolling on down the avenue. He was probably laughing to himself all the while. Soon I saw a little cloud of smoke coming out of his bag. Satisfied, I decided to be on my way before he caught on, and I headed for my sound check at the Rocker Room.

In May, Johnny called to tell me he had put together a new band, this time with Wayne Kramer from MC5.

"Wow, that's great!" I told him, knowing right away that this was going to be something spectacular.

"We're gonna start recording a few demos, but we need a drummer. Do you want to join in?"

"I wouldn't want to dump The Senders, but we have nothing else booked this week, so sure. Where are you?"

"We're in Ann Arbor, next to Detroit."

"Ann Arbor? I've been there—it's far. How do you want me to get to Ann Arbor?"

"We're buying you a plane ticket right now. We've got this guy taking care of everything, he's our . . . manager. I'm gonna call him. Can you come tonight? We'll pick you up at the airport. That guy has a house for me, and I can put you up. You'll see, it's great! I'm here with Julie and the kids."

So that evening I took a plane to Ann Arbor, and Johnny and Wayne Kramer picked me up at the airport. I immediately felt that Wayne was a righteous dude—very funny and with a positive energy that was contagious.

"What are you gonna call the band?" I asked him in the car.

"Gang War!" he said with a big smile, studying my reaction.

My reaction was mostly that I was thrilled to meet him. I had been a fan of MC5 for a long time—and was particularly in awe of him and Fred "Sonic" Smith. They were so cool—the American Stones, the Detroit hoods. Manufacturing Center 5, Motor City 5, or even Marijuana Cigarette 5. They were the first group to have released a hit record in which they yelled out "Motherfuckers" and that was in 1969! MC5 had helped build the foundation of punk rock, as did their little brothers from Detroit: Iggy & the Stooges.

Johnny's house in Ann Arbor wasn't bad at all. It was big and didn't have the junkie atmosphere I'd expected. It was clean and filled with kids' toys and baby chairs. Julie was always very nice to me, and she and Johnny seemed quite happy at the time. We got to work that very evening, and we kept recording for three days straight. On the way to the studio, we picked up Wayne's friend Ron Cooke, a local bass player. Their manager had rented the studio; all he'd been able to find was this little room where they recorded ads and jingles. They'd never done rock 'n' roll before. When we arrived, the owner—a very straight-laced guy—panicked at the sight of us. He nervously asked that everyone show ID!

"You've got to be joking," the manager replied. "These happen to be very famous musicians: Wayne Kramer of MC5 from Detroit, and over there is Johnny Thunders from the New York Dolls."

He looked at Johnny and said, "Don't try any bullshit with me. My son was a fan of the New York Dolls. I'll get him, and we'll see about this!" He yelled out, "Billy! Come down for a minute, would you?" Their house was directly above the studio, and his son—a fat kid in Bermuda shorts—came out munching on a sandwich.

"This one," the father said, pointing at Johnny. "Is he in the New York Dolls?" The son came closer to take a better look, then exclaimed, in absolute shock, "Dad, that's Johnny Thunders! Their guitarist!" From then on, the atmosphere improved significantly. The owner called for his wife, and she came out with an Instamatic to take photos of themselves with Johnny. Hahaha! Such a Disneyland, Mickey Mouse-type picture to hang in the living room!

This fucking guy was always asking me questions about what was going on, like: "Why is he going to the toilet so much?" or "What's wrong with him?" Every ten minutes, he would say to me, with a desperate look in his eyes, "But he's singing completely flat—he can't sing!" to which I would always reassure him, "Ah, no, he sounds great!"

We recorded "MIA," one of Johnny's new songs. The other tunes were "I'd Much Rather Be with the Boys" by the Stones, "I'm Gonna Be a Wheel" by Fats Domino, and two other Johnny originals "Who Do VooDoo" and "Just Because I'm White (How Come You Treat Me Like a Nigger)" with it's sure-to-be-a-hit title. There was, of course, no rehearsal, but that wasn't really a problem. Wayne and his pal were pros, and by now I was used to this kind of thing with Johnny. He'd just look at you and say, "Just play Bo Diddley" or "Just play ta-ta-boom, ta-ta-boom, okay? One, two, three, four. . . ."

This project was brand new for both Wayne and Johnny, and you could feel their excitement. Sparks were flying—they were both on fire. It was magical.

I was sitting there at the drums, banging away, just thinking, *Pinch me!*

Johnny came back to the studio wearing the same ripped-up T-shirt every night. It must have been his new favorite shirt. The last day, the owner handed me a perfectly ironed and folded white T-shirt and said, "I understand that times have been hard, but it truly saddens me to see that this musician who was once so successful has nothing left to put on his back than this torn-up rag. Can you please give him this from me so he doesn't have to feel ashamed anymore?"

To this day I remain friends with Wayne, who really is a great guy. Getting to play with him was always a total joy. He once filled in for Wild Bill at the Peppermint Lounge, where The Senders were opening for the Cramps. They were recording their legendary "The Smell of Female" that night.

I loved Gang War, and I was certainly tempted to take them up on their offer to be their full-time drummer, but I couldn't leave my beloved Senders. I also told myself that with Johnny on board, that band might not last very long. What a strange idea. . . .

So I went back to New York to continue my life as a Sender, but I was overjoyed to have had the chance to participate in those sessions in Ann Arbor.

The Senders were starting to have drummer problems, too, actually. Tony was an absolutely fantastic drummer, but he drank way too much and it was discouraging. Finally, we were scheduled to play at CBGB one night, and when we were called onstage, there was no Tony! After a long and embarrassing wait and a lot of complaining from the club, he called on the phone, lit up like a Christmas tree. When I asked him where he was, he said he had no idea but that it would be wiser for him to stay there. So, I filled in for him on drums, but we were more than a little hurt. We sacked him, replacing him with Marc Bourset, who had played in the Victims, a band we really liked. Tony went on to join the Criminals, the New York Dolls' Sylvain Sylvain's new band, then ended up spending years with David Johansen during his Buster Poindexter period.

Marc Bourset, aka M. T. Heart, aka Little Moe Trucks, aka the Human Drumming Circus, was exactly that: Keith Moon American style, endless wells of energy, extremely funny but also dangerous. He raced stock cars on Sundays at Islip Speedway's Demolition Derby, where he totaled old cars for kicks. That was his hobby. Musically, Marc was into the exact same things as we were, and he knew a lot about old rhythm and blues. He also had a true passion for old B-movies. He could recite the entirety of *Psych-Out* or any of the others. He knew them all by heart. He was perfect for The Senders, and we knew it right away. He played drums full tilt and lived life the same way. In the end, he was going to be ten times more trouble than Tony ever was, drinking and drugging more than the rest of the band put together, but we didn't know that yet at the start of the summer of 1979.

All we knew was that we were hired to play for three weeks in Los Angeles, at the Troubadour, the Starwood, Club 88, and all around.

We stayed at the Tropicana, the famous motel where Jim Morrison and Janis Joplin, and later Tom Waits and Rickie Lee Jones, had all spent a good amount of time. We had a small apartment on the ground floor by the parking lot—our Hollywood Royal Suite. There was only one room, and it was filled with our equipment— amps and drum cases everywhere.

I loved the so-very-Californian early fifties splendor of the Tropicana, with its crappy pool, palm trees, and its cheap, decadent atmosphere. I thought for sure Jayne Mansfield would pop out from somewhere at any minute—headless!

As soon as we got to LA, however, our troubles began. The agent who had booked our shows—a very nice young woman—came to meet us at the Tropicana, arriving at the wheel of a luxury sports car. Marc was already seriously drunk, and he immediately jumped into the car and took off. We were trying to calm her down, assuring her that he was only joking and that he would bring it back right away, when he finally reappeared, then sped past us without stopping, blasting down Sunset Boulevard at over a hundred miles an hour. The girl turned green. He came around a second time, then a third, back and forth, faster and faster each time. She was starting to talk about calling the cops, so we tried to distract her with questions like, "Is the place we're playing tonight nice?" and "So, were you born here?" Finally, Marc seemed to realize that we were getting bored of his joyride, and he returned the car to the parking lot, got out, and said to the girl, "Nice ride, I'll take it!" before turning to me and adding, "What's the matter? You didn't sleep good?!"

I knew right away that Marc was going to get along with Bruce!

A few days after we arrived, there was a pool party at the Tropicana to celebrate the recent marriage between Nick Lowe and Carlene Carter, Johnny Cash's stepdaughter. We didn't know them and weren't invited, but we went anyway, near the end, as people were leaving. They left so much food behind—huge trays of fruit, crawfish, seafood, and cold cuts of all kinds. So we brought it all back to our royal suite! We weren't able to finish it all, and it rotted and stunk up our little apartment in no time—and also attracted an impressive army of ants.

We played three nights in a row at the Starwood with Levi & the Rockats, an excellent rockabilly band. The place was packed with pretty little California girls—all blond and tan—staring up at us, mouths open. We were as pale as could be and sickly looking, with our dirty black suits and our greasy DAs. But they loved us all! Levi Dexter, the singer, had come from England with two or three other British Teds. They went straight to Norfolk, Virginia—birthplace of Gene Vincent—intending to find a few other young rockabilly enthusiasts to join their group. Instead, they'd been surprised to find only fans of Lynyrd Skynyrd—none of whom gave a flying fuck about what they considered to be their grandparents' music! Haha! Right place, wrong decade! But they were able to find what they wanted in New York, and were now under the wing of Leee Black Childers, the Heartbreakers' ex-manager and one of the former bosses of Mainman, David Bowie's management company. Leee was one of my favorite characters at Max's—a very funny and wonderful guy. He came up with the idea of a promo for those LA shows, photographs in which The Senders and the Rockats posed as two rival gangs at the Griffith Observatory in Hollywood Hills. It was the site of the famous scene in *Rebel Without a Cause,* where James Dean gets in a knife fight with Dennis Hopper and his gang. Leee rented a house not far from the Tropicana, where he put up Levi and the whole band. We spent most of our afternoons over there with them, or with the Go-Go's, who were also really cool and lived right nearby. In addition to that, like good little tourists, we went sightseeing—for instance, we went to see the house where Sharon Tate was murdered and the ranch where Charles Manson lived with his girlfriends.

Hanging out at the hotel was a bit of a drag, especially because Moe's girlfriend insisted on calling every ten minutes. She was very suspicious of what we were doing in there, claiming to hear girls' voices in the background and endlessly accusing Moe of lying. He called New York one morning to tell her that everything was going fine, then a few hours later, someone knocked on the door. It was her! Apparently, she had jumped on the first plane to "surprise" him and catch him red-handed. She made a ridiculous entrance, absolutely furious, demanding to know, "Where is she?!" only to find him eating a sandwich in the kitchen. She did a quick but meticulous search of the apartment, before giving him a kiss, adding, "Surprise!"

We played at the Hong Kong Café with a local punk band called the Heaters. There was this one guy in front of the stage who kept spraying beer on Steve. Finally, when Steve was totally soaked, he handed me his bass, jumped off the stage, and chased the poor horrified guy out of the club. Then cool as a cucumber, he climbed back onstage and lit a cigarette, to our peals of laughter.

Backstage a little later, the guy politely approached Bill. "I play in the Heaters, the other band," he said. "I am truly sorry about pissing off your bass player. I hope he's not still mad." All the while, he was checking left and right, worried Steve might be nearby. When Bill told him not to worry, he got a bit more cocky, adding, "That guy didn't have to lose his cool like that! Here in LA, spraying beer on someone is an expression of punk friendship. That guy has no sense of humor."

Immediately, Bill snapped back, "No, you're the one with no sense of humor, asshole! In New York, it's an expression of friendship to chase a guy and beat him up!"

The following night at the Troubadour was fantastic. After the show, we met one of the musicians from Paul Revere & the Raiders, and he invited us to record a few songs at his studio on Venice Beach. We did so, and before the final mix, Michelle Phillips of the Mamas & the Papas came by to play tambourine for one of our songs. Unfortunately, we weren't there and we never got to meet her, but there is a recording of The Senders that features her!

During our three weeks in LA, we played constantly, and also did a taping of a TV show. One afternoon, we played at a millionaire's party for a film production company. The party was in a lavish garden, and there were magicians and acrobats, and a Mariachi band in sombreros and ponchos strolled among the guests—all of whom were wearing tuxedos and elegant gowns. Also on the bill was the Know, a new band with Gary Valentine—who had just left Blondie.

Just before we went onstage, we were told that the guests were hoping to see some examples of that punk movement they'd been hearing so much about. I was still drunk from the night before, so I didn't hesitate to make them happy. I told the band to play as loud as we could, and swearing more rudely between each song, I sprayed beer on all the guests, gesturing like I was jerking off, while Marc threw half of his drum kit. The audience was completely outraged, so I told the band to pump up the volume even more. It was hilarious. One old lady even fainted right in front of the stage. Other bands had young women in miniskirts fainting at their shows; we had old ladies in evening gowns! Still, it's better than nothing. So, for one sunny afternoon in Hollywood, at the request of the public—who in this case were a bunch of old farts in suits—we were a tad more punk than usual.

That same evening, we played at another club—though I forget the name. I do remember it was pretty far from the hotel. We had two cars at our disposal—not counting our agent's sports car—and after the show, while I was at the bar flirting with a blond who looked like Veronica Lake, everyone assumed I'd gotten into the other car and they all drove off without me. When I finally came out of the club and realized I had no ride, I ran back inside to ask that girl to give me a lift. But she was gone too. There was no one left. I waited around, hoping someone would realize I wasn't there and come back for me, but to be honest, I had my doubts. . . . To top it all off, it was five in the morning and I didn't have a dime on me. The hotel was on the same street as the club—Sunset Boulevard—and it was a straight drive, but too far to walk. After sitting there for a while, I eventually decided to try hitchhiking. I was picked up almost immediately by two large Black guys in a Ford Mustang. As I got in the car, I started to thank them, when one guy cut me off to ask the other, "Do you smell something funny?" I started sniffing around to see what they were talking about when the other one answered, "Yeah, you're right, it stinks like whitey in here. It smells like a little stinking white shit!"

Holy fuck! I almost crapped my pants. *Mommy! Mommy! I'm dead!* I told myself, trying to keep my terror from being too obvious. I finally said, "Here's my hotel. I can get out here. Thanks again, you guys." They dropped me off without a problem, bursting into laughter as I got out of the car. I started laughing too, relieved that I was still alive.

Steve, Basile, Bill, Phil, and Marc, 1980

CHINESE ROCKS

New York, 1979

WE CAME BACK TO NEW YORK to the news that Max's was launching their own record company—Max's Kansas City Records—and they wanted us to do an album with them. The Troggs—the legendary British band that had brought us "Wild Thing"—was also going to be recording an album for their label. We accepted their offer right away and happily signed the contract promising us a minimum sum of *one dollar!* All four of us asked in unison if they had any quarters. On the other hand, we were also guaranteed all the free dinners we wanted at the club's restaurant downstairs. With the exception of Bill, we were all so skinny that they knew damn well they could get us with free food!

We recorded *The Senders Seven Song Super Single,* produced by Peter Crowley, the club's manager, and we were pretty happy with the result. The record was released as a twelve-inch vinyl with a magnificent black-and-white cover. We would bring it with us whenever we went to Max's so the waiter could verify our identities and we could order lobster without having to pay for it. One night, one waiter actually asked Marc to make the same expression as on the album cover, because he couldn't recognize him. The guy should have, because they'd decorated the walls of the bar upstairs with big framed photos of all the bands, and the first one you saw when you walked in was a fantastic shot of The Senders. We had become one of the club's favorites.

Peter Crowley invited me to play harmonica for the Troggs' album, but they must not have been too thrilled with my work, because when the record came out, I wasn't on it! We signed a one-year management contract with Frank Yandolino and his partner Michael Lang. Michael was the guy who had organized Woodstock—the little guy with curly blond hair you can see on a motorcycle in the movie. He also managed Joe Cocker. We might have thought that glory was right around the corner, but in reality, we didn't think much about it. We didn't give a damn. We were living in a fucking movie. Most of all, it was essential to us that we keep our artistic integrity, rather than becoming someone else's puppet—even if the pay was better. After all, we weren't particularly ambitious; we were perfectly content to be in our own little trip, and we felt that we had already made it, since we'd successfully avoided working nine-to-five office jobs like most of our friends were doing. Why let some idiot in a polyester suit ruin everything?

But we now had a manager who could negotiate with the enemy, which seemed like a good idea, since our ridiculous rebel attitude wasn't going to get us very far. In the meantime, we played everywhere. Constantly. Max's, CBGB, Hurrah's, the Peppermint Lounge, the Mudd Club, Rock Lounge, the Rocker Room, Tracks, Heat, Great Gildersleeves, Studio 10, A-1, Irving Plaza, the Orpheum Theater. In the suburbs too: My Father's Place, Dirt, Maxwell's. We played Brooklyn, Queens, Long Island, New Jersey, Connecticut, Massachusetts, Pennsylvania. . . . From Philly to Boston, nonstop. The Senders would go back to Boston at least once a month to play at the famous Rat. We often played there with the Real Kids, stars of the Boston underground and a great fucking band. John Felice, their guitarist and singer, would put us up at his place, and there were always a few girls who wanted to take us home, including a pretty ugly one we called "Potato Face." Potato Face was actually really nice. She had a Mod look, wearing white plastic miniskirts and sunglasses, with her coal black hair in a Cleopatra haircut. She would tell all her girlfriends about us and eventually started a little fan club. The audience at the Rat was very cool, and we always felt welcome there. They drank a lot in Boston, and it was pretty wild. I was always glad to go back to Boston—it felt like my "American hometown."

There was one night at the Rat that we felt we were so good, the sound was so perfect, and the energy in the room was so unbelievable, that I remember it was actually magic. For a few minutes there, we might have been the best rock 'n' roll band in the world, and the audience knew it—you could see it in their eyes. We had them by the balls. I don't know why—it's hard to explain—but I never forgot that show. Perhaps you have to have been in a rock band to understand what I mean, but I believe it would be worth it to spend a lifetime onstage just to live those few seconds when all is right, when the band and the audience become *one*. Anyone who hasn't had the luck of experiencing that during their lifetime has missed out on something incredible: the real magic of rock 'n' roll mixed with the real magic of being young and drunk! We were beside ourselves—it was fantastic. After three glorious encores, Bill, drenched in sweat, collapsed onto a sofa, laughing his ass off, and declared, "We're the fucking Yardbirds, man! It's 1966 and we're the fucking Yardbirds! Hahaha!"

We could have gone home to New York right then and there. It would have been the perfect evening. But *nooo*, why not stay a little longer and fuck everything up?

By four in the morning, the room was still loaded with people. Not as loaded as we were, though—particularly Marc. There was this one hippie girl—a Deadhead, perhaps—who was totally into Bill. A little chubby chick, who just had to have our guitarist! She kept trying to invite him over, but he didn't seem to particularly interested in her.

"We're all in the same car," he explained. "We can't leave each other! How will I get back to New York with a Twin-Reverb amp and two guitars if those assholes leave without me?" She then turned to me and asked if we would like to come over for salad.

"Salad?" I said as politely as I could. "I don't think that's a good idea. We're all smashed—look at that bunch of nuts, do you really want them in your home?" We could have easily gone to crash at the Real Kids' or at Potato Face's, and what did she want with a bunch of greasers drunk out of their minds, anyway? Was she that crazy about Bill that she couldn't see the state we were in? Was she out of her mind or what? But she insisted and Bill finally talked us into going to her place. He climbed into her car, and we followed them through Boston as best we could. We sat down in her kitchen, and she started pulling out eggs, tomatoes, and all the rest. Then she started telling us all about the Grateful Dead. The Grateful Dead?! Was that sheer provocation or what? They were the incarnation of everything we most loathed: old San Francisco hippies, the dreariest band in the world. Precisely *the* name to avoid! As soon as she turned her back, Marc threw an egg across the kitchen. It exploded against the wall, then slowly started trickling down to the floor. Things snowballed from there. We all grabbed everything she had just put on the table and started lobbing them at each other: tomatoes, lettuce, cucumbers.

"Can we help?" Bill asked.

The girl seemed to think it was funny, which naturally encouraged us to fuck around even more. Steve went into the living room and put on a record, with the volume up high: the Stones' *Exile on Main Street*. Marc came out of the bathroom holding a tube of shampoo to his crotch, spraying white liquid everywhere, and shouting, "Shit, I'm coming! Look, I'm coming!" Bill found a few beers in the fridge and helped himself, throwing one to Marc.

"If you can, don't drink all the beers. They belong to Bob, my roommate!" the girl said.

Her what?! She told us she had a roommate, but he worked the night shift and wouldn't be home until around seven in the morning. We went searching for Bob's room and started putting everything we could find into his bed. We didn't realize what time it was and figured we'd be long gone by the time he got back. Marc emptied an ashtray onto the sheets, then threw in a little salad.

"Oh, man, you guys, that's fucked up," I laughed at them.

While Bill was flirting with the girl in the kitchen, we started making more and more of a racket in the living room. Marc turned the record all the way up, playing "Happy," then "Turd on the Run," and "Ventilator

Blues," and we all started shouting, "Some kind of ventilator. . . . What you gonna do about it? What you gonna
do?" Then we screamed at the top of our lungs: *"Gonna
fight it, gonna fight it!"* and pounded our feet on the
floor in rhythm. The girl should have thrown us out but
she just kept laughing. She hadn't seen what we'd done
to her roommate's bed yet.

Then somebody pounded on the door. It was the
downstairs neighbor—a cute girl—and she demanded,
"Are you completely crazy or what? Do you realize the
racket you've been making? It's past 5 a.m.—enough
already!" Marc took one look at her and decided to go
cruise her in the stairs, trying to convince her to join
the party. Goofing around, I closed the apartment
door on him, locking him out. The neighbor didn't
find Marc's advances funny at all, and she ran back to
her place, threatening to call the cops. Stuck in the
hallway, Marc started pounding on the door, shouting,
"Very funny, you guys! Open the door, you assholes!
Open the fucking door or I'll knock it down!!!" Our
hippie girl ran to open the door at the exact moment
Marc kicked it in. The door went flying into her face,
bam! She fell to the floor. There were a few hooks on
the back of the door and one of them had hit her
square in the middle of the forehead. She sat up,
holding her face in her hands, and we saw blood running between her fingers. *Shit!* Now we really had
crossed the line. Immediately, Steve pulled off the

record, and we all jumped on her. "Holy shit! Are you all right? What happened? Are you okay?!" She clearly wasn't: she had a hole in her forehead and it was gushing blood. We were sure she would finally get pissed off, but no, this girl was unflappable! She just kept smiling, blood running down her face, telling Marc—who was bending over backwards apologizing—that it wasn't his fault, that it was an accident, and that he shouldn't worry. That poor hippie girl was a fucking saint, and we felt like total schmucks.

"She probably needs a few stitches," said Bill. "I'll take her to the hospital." We put some ice in a dish towel and stuck it against her head, and Bill took off with her to the emergency room.

We found ourselves sitting there, mortified and ashamed, as we looked over the damage we had done to the apartment. It was spectacular. There was food everywhere, on the floor, in the kitchen, in the living room, in the roommate's bed. . . . *The roommate! Shit!* He was going to be home any minute now—and he was going to find three strange guys, shit everywhere, blood on the floor, and no hippie girl! Realizing that we were going to get massacred, or at the very least arrested, we decided we would try to clean everything up before he got home—but it was impossible. We were sliding on the broken eggs, beer, shampoo, and all the other stuff we'd thrown around. On top of that, we were still too drunk to actually do any good. All we managed to do was to make matters worse. There was nothing to do. It was too late and we were fucked.

We waited in suspense. Who was going to come home first? Bill and the girl, or the roommate? And who was this roommate we would have to deal with? Maybe this Bob guy was a karate teacher, or a cop, or a Hell's Angel—or a hit man for the mafia! From the look of his clothes, he must have been pretty big. We absolutely had to get the hell out of there, but we couldn't leave without Bill. First of all, that would have been very mean, and second, he had the car. So we waited in the kitchen for what seemed an eternity. We debated the merits of waiting downstairs for Bill, just in case the roommate did come back first, but in the end, we figured that if there was no one there to explain to him what had happened, he would call the cops immediately, and things could only go downhill for us from there. So we decided we would stay put and tell him a version of the truth—that there had been a party and the girl had had a little accident and all those bastards who had messed up the apartment had left . . . except for us, who had stayed behind to clean up. And most of all, we had no idea who had gone into his room.

Suddenly, we heard someone unlocking the door. We froze, in absolute terror. Thank God, it was Bill and the girl. She had three stitches and a huge Band-Aid on her forehead. She was still smiling, though.

"I'm going to lie down," she said, taking Bill by the hand and leading him into her room. She closed the door.

"Shit! Now they're gonna fuck!" Steve moaned.

"No way!" Marc cried. "It's ten to seven—run for your life!"

They both looked at me. "Phil, go get Bill—we're outta here!"

I opened the bedroom door just a little bit, peeked in, and saw through the darkness that they had just crawled into bed. "Bill," I whispered politely. "We're leaving!"

I turned and headed for the door so he wouldn't have a chance to argue. He came hurrying out of the bedroom, pulling up his pants, "Wait for me. Wait for me!"

After that, we were afraid to go back to Boston for a while. We felt really bad for the poor girl, though. We thought of sending her flowers or something, but ultimately decided it was probably best to disappear and let her forget about that night.

Meanwhile, back in New York, the shows went on. Max's, CB's, etc.

The bands at Max's and CB's got along pretty well. Everyone went to each other's shows. There was a spirit of friendly competition among the camaraderie. And of course, any time someone had anything nice to say about your band, they would immediately cut you to pieces as soon as you turned your back. It was always, "Wow! That was great, Tim—loved your show!" then, as soon as Tim was three feet away, "What a horrible fucking band. They suck!" But all in all, everyone was friendly.

Backstage at Max's, the walls that separated the dressing rooms were so thin that you could hear everything going on in the next room. We would yell things like, "Wow! Did you see who we're playing with tonight? They're fabulous!" while pretending to throw up, with someone adding, "Yeah, really good!" and miming jerking off.

After a show one night, we were casually smoking a joint backstage and listening delightedly to the band in the next room getting berated by their manager. They were Bon Jovi clones, but by the way he was screaming, you'd think they were a fucking football team. "You were horrible, hor-ri-ble!" he yelled. "We talked about this at rehearsal—the energy, where was the energy? And you fucked up at least ten times, always in the same spots! Horrible!!" Then, much to our surprise, he added, "Why can't you be more like that other band, those Senders? Now, that's a band!"

We all exploded into laughter, and I nearly choked on the joint.

"Shhh," hissed Steve. "It's too good to be true."

"It's good advice. He's right!" Marc whispered.

"That's true. If we were a band, we'd want to be more like us."

"We should hire that manager."

"No way. They're putting us on. They also have a secret backstage code."

"Maybe, but theirs is much more elaborate. . . ."

We had T-shirts made: black, with The Senders logo in magenta. We sold them at shows and at Rebop. When summer came, Marc had the excellent idea of giving them to all the Bowery bums panhandling, usually drunk out of their minds, in front of CBGB. It was our advertising campaign. Our "models" seemed glad to have something clean to put on as they wiped wind-shields at red lights, while we were happy for the free advertising they so graciously gave us twenty-four seven.

I did all the graphics for our posters, which we would get printed on Canal Street. They were adorned with slo-gans like, YOU CAN'T OD ON R&B or DON'T GO COLD TURKEY FOR THANKSGIVING. There were no computers to do the lettering in those days, and you had to scratch each letter one by one from clear plastic sheets to print them on the poster. It never worked; in the end, all the info would get completely fucked up and there would be different amounts of space between each letter. That may be how the "pUnK pOsteR" style started. For a while, we paid a guy to put our posters up all over the Lower East Side, but we figured he was probably throwing away half of them so he could get home sooner, so we started putting them up ourselves. This involved walking around with a bucket of mixed paste and water, which was a drag, so we drove everywhere—spilling glue all over the seats as we stopped at street corners to hang flyers and have a smoke. What a joke! Once, a little hardcore punk asked if he could have a little bit of glue to solidify his Mohawk! Another one—who looked fucking insane—asked if he could have a sip.

"It's industrial glue," I said, "and we dropped the brush in dog shit!"

"Really? Great!" he said, as he plunged his hand into the bucket then swallowed a big gulp of it. If he didn't die, he must have gotten pretty constipated.

Thursday and Friday nights often turned into "poster wars." We would just be wrapping up three hours of postering, only to discover that some lame band had covered up *all* of our posters, because they were playing the same night. So, we'd rip down all of theirs. In order to avoid a big confrontation or an all-out rumble, when we spotted a band covering up our posters, we would just discreetly follow them with the car. We would pull down their posters as soon as they disappeared around the corner, laughing at the thought of their faces when they discovered their posters had already vanished! By then, the glue on ours would be dry, and they wouldn't be able to tear them off. Haha! The best thing to do was to put them up at 6 a.m. and hope we were the last coat; after all, it was illegal to put up posters on the streets of New York. We did get caught by the police once, but when the cop saw the posters, he offered to let it slide in exchange for one of them, saying he was a big rock fan. "Take three and we're good for the year," said Steve.

We ended a night of putting up posters by throwing glue at each other . . . which was fun for a while but ended with me in the hospital the next day. One of my eyes was completely glued shut, and I couldn't open it at all. They had to pry my eyelids open with pliers like in *A Clockwork Orange*, spraying my eye with a solution to dissolve the glue. Charming. . . .

One day, I noticed a phone number written in very small print at the bottom of an old cardboard poster from the fifties a friend had given me. That poster was beautiful. It read: *Hilton Hotel, Los Angeles, October 14, 1957, from 8 PM to midnight, $2.75 The biggest show of stars: Jerry Lee Lewis, Fats Domino, Little Richard, Chuck Berry, Lavern Baker, Bo Diddley, Eddie Cochran, Bill Hailey & the Comets, and the Everly Brothers.*

I wondered if the company that printed the poster could possibly still be in existence, so I decided to call the phone number to find out. Some lady in Indiana answered.

"You're looking for who? A poster printer? Ah . . . you know, there was a printing company at this number, but they moved to the other side of town at least twenty years ago. They were called . . . hmm . . . Show Print.

Yes, that's it, Show Print." I called information in Earl
Park, Indiana, and found Show Print right away. Not
only did they still make those posters, but they were
really cheap too. I ordered a bunch, and they sent them
over by mail. Show Print had survived by doing boxing
and wrestling posters. Cardboard posters with black
and white pictures of Mexican pro-wrestlers on rainbow
backgrounds in horrible orange, yellow, green, blue . . .
a dream! Not only were those cardboard posters beautiful, but they were also much easier to put up on the
street. No more need to mess around with glue—we
simply stapled them two by two around lampposts and
trees. It was so much easier, and on top of that, we were
the only ones in New York to have those kinds of posters.
Unfortunately, someone finally noticed the little phone
number printed at the bottom of each one—just like I
had—and we got copied.

We also had buttons made, black and magenta, like
our T-shirts. We were flattered to see that John Felice of
the Real Kids was wearing one on his leather jacket on
the cover of their new record.

The Heartbreakers had buttons with the title of their
song "Chinese Rocks" on them. I thought that was a
great idea, but we didn't have the money to make more
buttons. Rebop had a few boxes of old fifties buttons
with weird little slogans on them, so I figured why not
write songs that used those slogans as titles? That way, I
would automatically have buttons to go with them!

That's how everybody ended up wearing buttons with the title of our latest hit, "I'm a Stranger Here Myself."

"Wow! You have buttons that go with your songs?"

"No, we have songs that go with our buttons—just don't tell anyone!"

Rehearsing at Steve's loft was starting to become a problem. The upstairs neighbor, who had let us do whatever we wanted, moved out, and two real unfriendly heavyset Puerto Ricans took his place.

I was alone at the loft one day, when one of them knocked on the door. "How ya doing?" he said. "I wanted to ask you something. That music you're playing, is that punk rock?"

"Um, no it's just rock, blues. . . ."

"Really? Are you sure? Because they were talking about that new thing on TV—punk rock—and they were saying that this music brings out violence in people, that it can even make you want to kill someone after a while, and when I hear you guys play, that's exactly what I feel!"

We decided to start rehearsing somewhere else. We rented a rehearsal space at the Music Building on 7th Avenue—a building that lived up to its name. Eleven stories of rehearsal studios—three per floor. A fucking band-practice factory!

One night, as we were packing up our stuff after a show somewhere on Long Island, I noticed Bill was carrying some large object wrapped in a blanket.

"What the hell is that?"

"It's the fish!" he said, trying to maneuver it into the trunk of the car.

He had stolen the big stuffed fish that hung above a door in the club.

"You're crazy! They're gonna see that it's missing."

"Gimme a break. You stole a fucking porcelain cat!"

"Yeah, but not from the club where we were playing. You don't shit where you eat." I laughed.

The fish ended up on the wall of our rehearsal studio on 7th Avenue. This studio was great. We rented it by the month, but since we weren't playing there every day, we sublet it to two other bands; we tricked each of them into paying half the rent, which let us use the space for free. We could have rented it to five other bands, not practiced at all, and made a whole bunch of money—we could have dropped the music and started a career in real estate!

Marc had painted *HE-MEN, WOMEN HATERS CLUB* in big white letters on the door of our studio. It came from the old TV show *The Little Rascals*; the titular characters had that same slogan painted on the door of their tree house. Swans—a crazy experimental band—were in the studio next to ours, and at the end of the hallway was Madonna, who wasn't famous yet. She flirted with me in the elevator a few times, but I thought she was tacky, and besides, I was married. At the time, she dressed like Pat Benatar, in black-and-white zebra-print tights with yellow knitted legwarmers over them. She was very . . . disco.

I have a theory about this: God was watching The Senders rehearse one night and, thinking we were cool, He decided to throw His almighty magic power unto us, pointing His holy finger toward our studio and instantly sending a great white lightning of success in our direction. But even God isn't perfect, and he doesn't aim so well . . . he missed us by only a couple of feet and the great white lightning landed on Madonna, who was waiting for the elevator!!

On top of that, I bet she still has no idea, because she's never thanked us or nothing.

Heading to rehearsal one night, I spotted a drunk businessman throwing up in the doorway of a building. I assumed he was a basketball fan coming out of Madison Square Garden, a little further down the avenue. It wasn't an unusual sight.

Poor guy, I thought. Given the state he was in, he was sure to get mugged—especially at this hour, in this neighborhood. Besides, he looked like he wasn't doing so good. He was doubled over, gripping the wall in front of him, and his wallet was sticking out of his back pocket. The only thing missing was a little sign saying HELP YOURSELF. I was hesitant to get involved as I thought he might be dangerous—given how loaded he was—and kept on walking. I was surprised to see him again the next day, in the exact same spot, still retching.

"This guy throws up here everyday?" I asked the doorman of the Music Building.

"No, he's a cop," he said, laughing. "And he isn't drunk at all. As soon as someone grabs his wallet, he spins around with his gun. There are three others in a car across the street. They bust about a dozen guys in an hour or two, and they throw them in a van parked around the corner so they don't have to go back and forth to the station every ten minutes. They leave when the van is full."

Those undercover cops were amazing. I once witnessed a mugging in the subway, during which a Hassidic Jew, a construction worker, and a rapper all pulled out their guns yelling, "Police!" I also once saw a little schoolgirl in Brooklyn slam a huge Puerto Rican guy against a wall, shouting in her walkie-talkie, "I got him! We're at the corner of Jay Street and Fulton. I need reinforcement!" Or maybe I saw that on TV—I can't remember! Anyway, it made me wonder if everyone around me was a cop. . . .

We were talking more and more about adding a new guitar player so we could once again be five—just like we were in the beginning. Rolling Stones style, which makes for a great sound. We were doing a sound check at Max's one afternoon, when a kid with a suitcase in one hand and a guitar in the other walked right up to me and said, "Basile Nodow!" He stuck out his hand and added that he had just arrived from Oklahoma City and that he had come to see us play after reading an interview in which we said great things about Dr. Feelgood, his favorite band! He asked us if he could plug in his guitar and play a song with us during the sound check. We liked his style a lot and invited him to come up and play a song during the show, too. He must have really knocked us out, because after a short meeting backstage, we unanimously agreed to hire him on the spot, before he could even drop off his luggage at the hotel.

After the show, Joe Strummer of the Clash, who was visiting from London, insisted on meeting with us. He really liked our music and told me that before the Clash he played in the 101ers, a pub rock band, and that he loved old American Black R&B just as much as I did. I didn't often meet anyone as cool or as interesting as Joe, and I offered him a drink right away—a Sender, of course, for which I didn't have to pay!

A little later, I was hanging out upstairs in the dressing room with Risé, waiting for Peter Crowley to count the money and pay us, when Bill came running up, yelling, "Phil, come quick! Steve's getting beaten up downstairs!"

A rumble! Shit! I had just smoked a joint, so talk about bad timing. I would have much rather talked about the universe or watched TV, but this seemed urgent. I grabbed my brass knuckles from my bag—they went perfectly with the rest of my getup. Brass knuckles are illegal in New York, but I'd recently seen a very funny ad in a biker magazine that read: *Magnificent Brass Paperweight, exact replica of classic Brass Knuckles!!* Haha! I figured they might be good to have in case of trouble, given where I lived. I wasn't particularly fond of switchblades—especially after what happened to Johnny Blitz—so, for ten bucks, I ordered a "paperweight."

I grabbed my paperweight and ran downstairs. I found Steve at the bottom of the stairs, near the front door, fighting three pretty big guys. Punches were flying in all directions. Two of his opponents held broken beer bottles, which they were using to hit Steve. Where were those fucking bouncers when you needed them? Without thinking about it too much, I grabbed one of the guys from behind, putting my arm around his neck like I had learned as a kid in judo class. Then I started to consider my situation, *I'm holding this guy here, and he doesn't look too happy about it, and I'm gonna have to let him go eventually and then he's gonna kill me!* Which is a terrifying thought—especially when you've just smoked a joint. So I let him go and quickly climbed backwards a few steps so I could be on higher ground before he turned around—which he did right away, real pissed. Immediately, I kicked him in the face and sent him flying into the doorframe, causing everybody to fall onto the sidewalk outside. Bill jumped on them, too. I pulled my weapon from my pocket, slipped it onto my hand, and grabbed one of the guys by the hair just as he was furiously stabbing Steve in the back. I clocked the shit out of him. It was the first time I'd ever used the thing, and I couldn't believe how good it was. The guy collapsed on his knees in front of me like a bag of potatoes. Blood poured down his face. I must have broken his nose. I'd just smoked pot and certainly it hadn't been my desire to seriously hurt anyone! Not to mention the fact that I'd never really been in a fight before, and immediately I felt real bad. As ridiculous as it may seem, I could think of nothing better to do than to ask him, "Are you okay?" Of course, he thought I was joking and that I was being totally arrogant and sarcastic. He looked at me, horrified, as if I were the worst bastard in the world, a sadistic maniac à la *A Clockwork Orange*. Right then, I felt a hand fall heavily on my shoulder. I turned around only to discover it was a cop, in full uniform. He immediately ripped the brass knuckles from my hand, handcuffed me, and threw me into the back of his car.

Steve and the guy I punched were taken to the hospital, and the two other guys and I were taken to the police station, where I was handcuffed to a chair. Suddenly, I heard someone yell, "I saw everything! I saw everything!" It was Wayne County, the Electric Chairs' drag-queen singer, who had broken Handsome Dick

Manitoba's shoulder. She had just strode into the station, screaming and shouting, saying that she was a witness and that she had come to set me free. Good Lord!

Unfortunately, the police station was only a few blocks away from Max's and everyone decided to come save me! One nut after another, they all descended upon the station. Neon Leon, with his blond wig, reeking of pot; a few groupies in spandex with makeup everywhere; Mikey Zone of the Fast, who entered the station with two pencils in his ears and two up his nose. . . . The circus had come to town. I sank a little further into my chair with each new person who showed, but hey, it was nice of them all the same.

In the end, it appeared as though the fight had been more or less Steve's fault. Completely wasted, he had gone looking for trouble—for no reason he could remember—and he found these three guys from Queens. It went bad quickly. He must have been really drunk, because that wasn't his style at all. I was arrested for assault with an illegal weapon. At six in the morning—three hours before going to court and being told my fate—Risé found me a lawyer.

Before seeing the judge, I was taken "downtown" to the general detention center for criminals in transit. I was thrown in a cell with about ten other losers, including a few fucked-up businessmen in suits, two or three Puerto Rican bikers, and the two guys we had fought against! The one I'd kicked in the face was sporting an impressive black eye. He stared at me from the other end of the cell, and then slowly got up and came over to me. He pulled a pack of cigarettes from his pocket and offered me one. I knew it had to be a setup and that I was sure to get mine any minute, but since I didn't have much choice and I did want a cigarette, I took a chance and accepted his offer. He sat by me, offered me a light, and started to apologize for all that had happened. While he was at it, he told me that he was already on probation; if Steve pressed charges against him and his friends, he would be sent back to jail for a long time. He said he would be very grateful if I would talk to Steve about it. Sure, this guy had attacked Steve with a broken beer bottle, but seeing the shiner I'd already given him, I accepted his request. Anyway, it wasn't like I was going to tell him to go fuck himself while I was still locked in a cell with him and his pal. After awhile, we started chatting about music, and we more or less forgot why we were there in the first place.

Then we were called to see the judge. Their other friend did indeed have a broken nose. Steve was covered with stitches, with cuts just about everywhere on his chest, back, hands, and forearms, but none were particularly deep or serious. Being as cool as he was, and admitting he had provoked his attackers, he didn't press any charges. In exchange, he asked that the guy with the broken nose refrain from pressing charges against me, thereby keeping my cellmate with the black eye from being sent back to jail. My lawyer managed to get my weapons charge dropped, explaining that I had bought the brass knuckles legally and acted only with the intention of helping Steve, who could have been killed—which was the truth, and which put me officially, or at least personally, in the category of a superhero.

From behind his desk, the judge was less than impressed by my heroism. He addressed me personally and said, "I don't welcome in *my* court delinquent foreigners who come to commit crimes in *my* city. Very nice to meet you, mister. Next time I see you, I promise you will be sent right back to France!"

I didn't ask for my paperweight back.

At the time, we had a Mexican roadie named Lalo, who was small and skinny and had a face full of acne. But he was a really sweet guy, and he would drag our equipment around without saying a word but always with a little smile. He was shy to the point that he could have passed for "simple." One night, just before a show, I got to Max's and found everyone in a panic. They told me Lalo's little apartment on Lafayette Street had burned down the night before. A terrible fire. Everything had been reduced to charcoal and ash, and worst of all, no one had seen Lalo since, and the firemen weren't giving any information about survivors.

We started to set up our equipment ourselves, and still no sign of Lalo. Where could he possibly have been last night other than at home? He was such a loner. What had happened to him? Was he dead? And what a horrible way to die, too. . . .

The evening started with Buzz & the Flyers onstage, but we were all just sitting, waiting on the third floor, stunned. We couldn't believe it. Damn it! Lalo was so nice—it was a complete shock. . . .

It was just as we were about to get onstage that Lalo appeared. He casually strolled in backstage and seeing us, he said shyly, "Sorry I'm late. Sorry, you guys!"

"*Lalo!!*" we all screamed, jumping all over him. "*You're alive!* We were so fucking scared, Lalo! Are you all right? What happened?"

"Oh, umm . . . I forgot there was a show tonight. I'm sorry . . . really sorry!"

"Are you kidding? We're the ones who are sorry, Lalo. We heard the news. . . . It's really horrible. We can put you up if you want. Don't worry about anything. What happened?"

"Umm . . . what?" he asked, bewildered.

The rest of us exchanged looks, all starting to think the same thing.

Steve tried again. "Your apartment, Lalo. What happened?"

"My apartment?"

"Yes, your apartment. Where did you sleep last night?"

"Umm . . . at this girl's house. I have a girlfriend, well . . . I think I do. I met her after the show the other night . . ."

"You're coming straight from her place, aren't you?"

"Yes . . ." he admitted. "But I had also forgotten that there was a show tonight, I'm sorry."

We were all so relieved that he was alive, and besides, the whole scene was so absurd that we all started cracking up.

"Lalo," I said, trying in vain to keep a straight face. "Your apartment burned down, you do know that, don't you?"

"Yeah, yeah, really funny. I'm sorry I'm late!" he said.

"No, we're not joking, your apart—" I started laughing so hard I couldn't finish my sentence. The rest of the guys were even worse, completely delirious—probably about to piss their pants. Of course, the more we tried to restrain ourselves, the worse our hilarity got.

"Sit down and listen. It's not a joke," I told him, trying with all my might to stay composed . . . at which point we all exploded again, ten times worse, practically rolling on the floor. I was laughing so hard the tears were streaming down my face.

"Lalo! Hahahaha! Hoho! Your apartment burned down!"

"Yeah . . . I got it. Very funny."

He had no idea about the fire, and the more we insisted, the more he thought it was a bad joke. Of course, the way we were telling him such terrible news was not especially convincing.

All of a sudden, we heard Peter Crowley yelling downstairs, "Hey, Senders! We're waiting for you onstage!"

We apologized to Lalo for giggling so much, swearing it was just a nervous reaction, but that his apartment really did burn down and that we were very sorry.

All he said was, "And I'm the Queen of England!"

Before beginning our first song Steve said to me, "Man, he's really gonna be upset when he realizes we weren't kidding."

"I hope his girlfriend has a nice place!"

Between 1980 and 1981, The Senders played an average of four shows a week in New York and its suburbs. I'd been practicing the guitar, and soon I was good enough to write all the band's songs on it. I also started playing harmonica, and I made quick progress by playing along to Little Walter's records. Plus, I played the harmonica onstage every night.

Our stage show was becoming a little crazier every night. Lalo would discreetly dump a whole bag of flour on the cymbals before the show, so that the whole stage would disappear under a white cloud when Marc started playing. It never failed to create the right atmosphere. We would walk onstage carrying bags of streamers, which we'd throw to the audience so they could throw them back on us later. That always went over well. If you give your audience things to throw at you, they will gladly oblige. So don't give them shoes or bricks. . . . The streamers would fly in all directions in a cloud of flour, and nobody would get hurt. Although nothing was actually choreographed, we did play one song—"Crazy Date"—during which we would lie down on the floor, and we asked everyone in the audience to do the same. Every now and then, people would give us little notes with song requests. I always loved to announce into the microphone, "Somebody has a special request, but we're going to keep on playing anyway!!"

Playing in bars night after night without spending too much time sleeping becomes its own universe of sorts. We *lived* in bars, onstage at night, with the flour, the streamers, and a seriously destructive R&B set. Nothing beats the feeling of a good audience that's right in front of you; it's actually ten times better than any large room with a high stage that keeps you from seeing jack shit. Being a bar band is an art, and one that we tried to perfect with an unlimited passion, progressively learning what tricks would cause just the right reaction. We weren't just there to play music; everyone in the audience had to go home soaked, messed up, worn out, or with us!

Joe Strummer came back to see us at Max's. Well, he came back . . . I don't know if it was specifically to see us or not, but we *were* playing that night. This time he was with Paul Simonon and his girlfriend Debbie, who I had gone out with before. It was really nice to see her again and she introduced me to Paul, who invited me over to their place on 3rd Avenue the next day. I spent the afternoon with them, smoking joints and listening to the reggae cassettes Paul was playing on his famous boom box. He was very happy to tell me about each song. Just like Joe, Paul was really cool, incredibly kind, very polite, and quite funny.

Unfortunately, the same could not be said of Mick Jones, their guitar player, who I met a few days later backstage at Max's before a Heartbreakers show. He was sitting at a table, tuning his guitar to get ready to play a song with them, when I went over to him and asked for a light. He just stared at me without saying a word. Figuring he was probably just as nice as the other two and was concentrating on tuning his guitar, I picked up the lit cigarette he had put on the edge of the table so I could use it to light mine.

He exploded. "Put it back on the table!!"

I was shocked, but politely told him I was just using it to light my cigarette and would put it back in a second. I was hoping he'd calm down, but instead, he got up in a fury and screamed, "*I said put it back!!!*"

Everybody was staring at us. I genuinely thought he was going to punch me. So immediately, I put his cigarette back on the edge of the table and went on my way, whispering to Johnny as I passed, "What an asshole!"

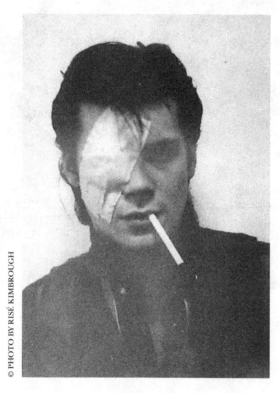

© PHOTO BY RISÉ KIMBROUGH

Phil, 1979

Phil, Steve, and Johnny, 1981

RUN, RUN, RUN

New York, 1981

I RAN INTO JOHNNY AT KIEV, the twenty-four-hour restaurant on 2nd Avenue where we often hung out after shows. It was four in the morning, and I'd come by to pick up a few cheese blintzes to take home, when I saw him sitting there. He was all alone and fast asleep in his food. I couldn't see his face but I recognized him by his hair and jacket. There was a roll of twenty-dollar bills at his feet, on the floor under the table. It had to be him!

"Hey! Johnny, wake up," I told him, shaking him by the shoulders. "You dropped your money. Good thing I saw you, or it would have gotten stolen. Are you all right?"

"Ehhh?" He slowly sat up, revealing an impressive black eye.

"Holy shit! Are you okay? Who did that to you? Johnny, your money is on the floor. Here, put it in your pocket."

"Heeyyyy, Flipper! Thanks, I must have fallen asleep," he said, still groggy. He started telling me that Julie's brothers had thrown him out of his own home. There had been a fight. He hit her, they hit him, everybody hit each other, but he couldn't remember in what order. He didn't know where to go. So I took him home with my cheese blintzes.

"Let's take a cab," he said. "We'll do a quick stop on Avenue D, all right? I'll give you some."

"Grand and Pitt," I told the driver. "But we have to stop on 3rd Street and Avenue D for a second to . . . return some keys."

When we got to Avenue D, we told the driver to stop at the corner, but he kept going, stopping instead in front of the abandoned building where Johnny was going to buy his dope. The security at the heroin dealer's building didn't want cars stopping in front of their place, and immediately a little Puerto Rican guy came up to the cab, waving a baseball bat.

"Move," he told the driver. "To the corner. There's a lot of cops tonight."

"Go fuck yourself, I stop where I want to. Who the fuck does this guy think he is?"

The guy slammed his baseball bat into the cab's hood. BAM!

"Move! Or I'll smash your windshield!"

"Move, come on, he's gonna kill us!!" we yelled from the backseat.

The cabbie finally took off, shocked, and then he didn't want to stop.

"*Stop! Stop!*" Johnny shouted. "Here! Hey, that's good, fucking pull over already!" Johnny jumped out. "I'll be right back, Flip."

"What's he doing?" the driver asked after a little while. "Look at my hood! Nothing but fucking crazies in this town, goddamn riffraff, no respect for nothing. They're lower than animals, you know? Human garbage, druggies, pimps. I got a gun. Do you know what I'm gonna do to this bunch of roaches, one day?"

I was starting to wonder if this guy was a friend of Robert DeNiro, when Johnny came back around the corner, hopping instead of walking, because he'd broken one of his boot heels during the fight with Julie's brothers. He tried to run too fast and stumbled, falling flat on his face on the sidewalk. A police car was slowly coming up the block, and it passed right by our cab while Johnny was on all fours trying to gather his bags of dope. By the time we got to my place, my blintzes were cold.

Johnny slept on the sofa for three days straight, only getting up to shoot up again. We only knew he wasn't dead because he snored like an elephant, and from time to time, we had to turn down the stereo to make sure he was still alive.

"Yeah, it's okay, I hear him," Risé would say.

He finally woke up and went to play at Max's. We went to see Mink DeVille at CBGB.

In November, Bruce decided to throw me a birthday party at his place. He invited the whole gang, as well as some others. Late that afternoon, I went to help him set up the apartment, and he greeted me with, "Lipper-LuLu! I just got back from the bakery. I got you a chocolate cake, but I left the candles on the counter and need to go back. Come with me and I'll let you pick out some other stuff to decorate your cake."

I agreed, promising to act surprised when I saw the cake at the party later.

At the bakery, I chose a few plastic planes and several Indians, essential for any good aviation- and Wild West-themed birthday cake. A cake good enough for Howard Hughes, you could say. As we were stepping out of the bakery, I just made it past the door when I heard a little click right by my ear. I turned around to see that there was a gun pointed right at my head!

"*Police! Freeze!*" yelled a second guy who was also aiming a gun at us; this one was behind a parked car. There was a third one, too, on the left, pointing his gun directly at Bruce. They were all in plain clothes. They jumped on us and threw us onto the hood of the car. One of the cops ripped the little white paper bag from my hand and demanded, victoriously, "What's in here, mister?"

"Umm . . . four plastic planes, and uh . . . three Indians . . . and some candles . . ." I told him.

Though he seemed to realize I wasn't kidding, he started to search me anyway. One of the others shouted into his walkie-talkie, "We got 'em! They were on 2nd Avenue." The third guy was getting very aggressive, asking us over and over, "Where is the gun?!" They handcuffed us, threw us in the back of one of their cars, and quickly drove us a few blocks away, where they stopped in front of a deli where two other police cars were already parked. Some guy, probably the cashier, came up to the car, looked in at us for a while, then turned to the cops and said, "No, it's definitely not them!"

"Shit man, good thing he wasn't blind!"

". . . or had Alzheimer's!" Bruce added, and we both started to laugh, discreetly.

They gave me back my planes and my Indians, and made a sort of apology. They explained that two guys matching our descriptions had just robbed a few stores in the area. The cops took off as suddenly as they'd appeared, still on the search for the right guys. We were a bit shaken, but nevertheless we went back home to decorate the cake.

The first guests arrived around 9 p.m., but the vibe wasn't very good. In fact, it was downright depressing. The guy Bruce had sent to Norfolk Street to get dope hadn't come back yet, and he'd been gone long enough that we were getting suspicious. There were about

twenty people in the living room and four on the stoop
outside, all nervously looking trying to get a glimpse of
him coming back. Bruce was getting freaked out, and
he was doing everything he could to keep things
gloomy, going so far as to stop the music so that no one
could dance, and yelling at the guests for being badly
dressed assholes! A few people were starting to put their
coats back on, even as others kept coming in, en masse.
The whole New York underground was there: Max's
posers, the "in" crowd, the has-beens and the would-
bes, the beautiful, the pathetic . . . but still no dealer.
Have you ever been to a party where junkies are waiting
for their dope? It's a little like a funeral, but way less
funny and way more uptight! Bruce was just about to
kick everybody out when suddenly, there he was! They
could see him far in the distance. He was quickly getting closer, they could see him fully now, and he was
grinning. Hallelujah!

Bruce put on James Brown's "Sex Machine" full blast
and a few champagne bottles were popped, as we all
ran toward Bruce's room to do the dope that had
finally arrived.

"Really good, isn't it?" Bruce said, slowly closing his
eyes and leaning forward.

He promptly collapsed on the floor.

"Fuck! He shot up three bags!" Cookie exclaimed,
looking up at me and David.

"Is he out of his mind?"

"Hey, Bruce, are you all right?" I shook him, but he wouldn't wake up. Shit! He'd OD'd.

"Help me get him up. Let's try to make him walk," I told the others. We dragged him back and forth as best we could, but to no avail. We laid him down on his bed and slapped him around a bit, but still nothing. Cookie put her hand on his chest, and I grabbed his wrist. We looked at each other in terror: there was no pulse. His heart had stopped. He was dead.

"Let's throw him in cold water—it might work," Cookie suggested. We carried him to the bathroom, pushing our way through the crowd of degenerates that had already filled up the apartment. Someone was in the bathroom but the door was unlocked. "Hey! I'm trying to piss!" he protested, as we threw him out of there. I locked the door while David and Cookie put Bruce in the bathtub and turned the cold water on full blast. The bathtub was slowly filling up, but Bruce still wasn't moving. We kept shaking him and slapping him, but it wasn't working. Meanwhile, a line for the bathroom was forming outside, and a few guys started banging on the door yelling things like, "Hey, ho! Come on, lovebirds, hurry up! Go rent a hotel room, goddammit!" and "Open the door, assholes, or I'm gonna piss on it!"

We looked at each other, none of us knowing what to do. The water kept rising and Bruce was still lying there, dead.

"Hey! Open the door, *hurry up!*"

"Sorry, this might take awhile. Go pee on a tree!" I yelled back through the door.

"But I have to shit!"

"It isn't cold enough—go get ice cubes!" Cookie said to me; she'd gone white, while Bruce was turning purple. "Hurry up!"

I ran out of the bathroom and found myself face to face with two very large and very drunk drag queens, who didn't look happy. "Ah! Finally, Romeo!" one said, while the other, glimpsing David and Cookie, started screaming, "My god! How many of them are in there?! It's an orgy!!" There were at least ten people waiting for the bathroom, and they all jumped on me.

"Hey, man, it's not *your* bathroom!" some little pimply punk said. I told him to fuck off.

"Shut up! Move!" I screamed, as I shoved him back with my arm, pushing my way through to the kitchen. "Happy birthday," another offered shyly. Same scene in front of the fridge, where I had stuck two large bags of ice cubes for the party. There was only a quarter of a bag left, and most of it was half-melted anyway. On my way back to the bathroom, moving as fast as I could, I actually started grabbing ice cubes from people's cups. I got stuck at the back of the line, where some jerk in a Hawaiian shirt told me, "Don't jump the line! We're all waiting here!" I went right through him, arms filled with ice cubes, also shoving aside the two drag queens and that same little pimply punk.

"Move! Move! Cookie, open the door, it's me!"

I slipped in the bathroom, while the people outside hurled insults at me, and threw all the ice cubes I had gathered into the bathtub, which was now full and where Bruce was still lying, dead. Cookie locked the door behind me, and I heard someone say, "He went to get rubbers?"

"No, ice cubes. His girlfriend's ass is on fire!"

The three of us were on our knees in front of the tub, paralyzed with fear, not knowing what to try next.

"Quick, we've got to do something! Coke! Who's got coke? Let's shoot him up with coke to give him a shock," I decided, running back out of the bathroom, shoving everyone aside again. I tried to locate Mike, a friend who had offered me cocaine maybe ten minutes earlier. I ran into the packed living room, where someone had just put on Devo's *Q: Are We Not Men? A: We Are Devo!* It was extremely loud and everyone was dancing in the dark. I switched the light on. People started yelling, but right away I spotted Mike and dashed over to him. "Mike, do you have any coke left?!" I demanded, desperately trying to scream over the music.

"Hey, Phil, great party!" he screamed back, continuing to dance like a fool. "Didn't you just tell me you don't like coke?"

"Yeah, gimme everything you've got! Hurry up! I'll buy it for twice the price—I'll give you anything you want!"

"Look, I'm a robot!" he said, as he took from his pocket a little plastic bag, which I instantly ripped from his hand.

"I'll explain later. Thank you!"

"Happy birthday. Leave me a little bit, okay?" I heard him yell, as I ran back toward Bruce's room to get a needle and a spoon. Rushing to the bathroom again, I heard one of the people in line laugh, "Look out! He's coming back!" They knew me by now, and they all cleared off. Once in the bathroom, I put *all* of Mike's coke in the spoon, mixed it with a little water, sucked it up into the syringe and stuck it directly into Bruce's arm.

Nothing. Still nothing. I pulled the needle from his arm and sat on the floor in a puddle of water.

"Hey, Romeo, open the door! It ain't funny anymore. I'm gonna pee my panties," yelled one of the drag queens.

"Me too!" came a chorus of about fifteen others.

"Salt!" said Cookie. "Water and salt! We should shoot him up with salt—let's try it. I read somewhere that it can work. Go get some salt! Hurry!"

I took off again as fast as I could toward the kitchen, cheered along by more insults, with most of the guests hiding their cups as they saw me. I ran right into Mike, who said, "Hey! You're running all around like a monkey. Did you snort the whole thing or what?!" I didn't bother to answer him as I ran and pushed everyone away from the bathroom door for a third time. I nearly got lynched as I banged on the door.

"Cookie, open up, it's me!" I screamed again. She mixed a little salt and water in the spoon and stuck the syringe right back into Bruce's vein. Nothing at all. I heard one of them yell from behind the door, "Cookie, open up, it's me!"

"Yeah, it's me too!" added another.

"All right, I'm calling an ambulance," I said, shaking like a leaf.

"We gotta throw everybody out and flush all the drugs down the toilet. The cops'll probably show up, too."

Suddenly, Cookie saw Bruce's eyelashes move a bit, then his mouth. It had worked! He was coming back! The salt had given his heart the jumpstart it needed. He opened his eyes and started to cough, then he shook his arms and legs, splashing water everywhere.

"Oh, my god! Thank you!!" Cookie screamed.

"At last! She came! Maybe we're gonna finally be able to pee," cried one of the drag queens behind the door.

Bruce got up, looking bewildered at the three of us in tears, on our knees in front of the tub. "What's fucking wrong with you guys?" he demanded. "Why'd you put me in the bathtub with my sharkskin suit on?"

"Bruce, you're alive! It's a miracle! You were dead!"

"Yeah, great, but you could've at least taken off my suit! It's gonna be ruined. That's really smart, I just bought it . . ." he grumbled, and stepping out of the tub, he opened the bathroom door and started for his room. We followed him, cheered on by the applause of the impressive crowd that was still waiting in line for the bathroom.

"This one was taking a shower fully dressed!" quipped one of the drag queens.

"Who invited that clown? Get outta my house!" answered Bruce, dripping all over the carpet. He took off his jacket and closed his bedroom door, then sat down at his desk. "Where did you put my spoon?" he asked me, pulling a few little cellophane bags out of a drawer.

"You're not going to shoot up again, are you?! Are you out of your mind? We just brought you back to life. You were dead, Bruce, for at least ten minutes," the three of us insisted.

"Yeah, but you know . . . honestly, I don't feel high at all anymore," he smiled, and soaking wet, he started to cook up his next fix.

Meanwhile, the Clash had become international stars. By far the biggest band from the punk movement. Seeing on the news that the Clash was adding a second week at Bond's Casino in Times Square, I decided to call our manager.

"Maybe they didn't hire all the bands to open up yet," I told him. "They saw us play at Max's, and I think they dug us. We should contact them about playing one of the shows with them."

"Yeah, right! Why not the Stones? Did they see you play? Do you want to open up for the Stones, too?"

"Yes!" I laughed. "But no really, we know them. I even hung out a bit with one of them last time they were in New York."

"You hung out with the Stones?"

"No, the Clash!"

"Phil, I am too busy for your nonsense." He hung up.

The next day, Steve and I were on motorcycle ride when we noticed a whole bunch of little punkettes in front of the Gramercy Park Hotel. "I bet that's where the Clash are staying," Steve said. A punk rocker was admiring his bike, so Steve asked, "Who are you all waiting for?"

"The Clash, man, the Clash!"

"Maybe I should ask about playing with them at Bond's. . . . I'll go look," I said, and without even taking the time to remove my helmet, I ran into the hotel. I decided to ask the concierge to deliver a message to the band from me, and I scribbled on a piece of paper, *Philippe, The Senders* and my phone number. Just then, a few girls started screaming, and I turned around to see Paul Simonon entering the hotel. I tried to get over to him, but he was already surrounded by a mob of fans asking for autographs. I was only able to make my way to him at the very last moment, just before he got into the elevator with his entourage; I slipped him my piece of paper, and blurted out, "How are you? We want to play with you at Bond's. Here's my num—" as the door closed.

I didn't think it would actually go anywhere, so I was surprised when I got a phone call from their manager that very evening. "Do you want to open up for the Clash at Bond's?" he asked, with a thick British accent.

"Yes, great! When?"

"Tomorrow night."

"All right, fabulous! How much money should I tell the band you'll pay us?" I asked him, before immediately panicking—figuring I'd just fucked the whole thing up.

But he didn't hang up on me. Instead, he said, "A thousand dollars—is that okay?" before adding, "Sound check is at four. See you tomorrow."

The next night, we found ourselves playing in front of eight thousand people. Before us, there was the rap band called Grandmaster Flash & the Furious Five. The graffiti artist Futura 2000 had been hired to spray-paint a huge metallic wall at the back of the stage as the Clash was playing. Sure to always be into the latest thing, the Clash really dug the hip-hop movement that was starting to explode in the clubs of the Bronx and Queens. They loved all the New York rappers, which, of course, did not translate to the rest of the average American punk rocker crowd, as most people still considered hip-hop to be a part of disco—the enemy, the worst music in the world! Grandmaster Flash was booed off the stage like you wouldn't believe. It was raining cans of Coke by the thousands. They got killed; it was pouring cans. The band and I looked at each other and said, "Fuck, we're next!"

We climbed onstage in almost total darkness. The audience thought we were the Clash and the room exploded with screams of *"Yyeeeaahhh!!"* It's true that in the dark we looked more like the Clash than Grandmaster Flash did. All the spotlights came on at once, and there was a comical moment when everyone in the room realized their mistake. Two or three cans of Coke came flying at us—including one that missed me by a couple of inches. *Shit!* I told myself. We had barely started the first song. . . . Fortunately for us, the cans stopped coming almost right away, and the crowd decided to give us a chance—probably glad that at least we weren't rapping. The show went beautifully. They couldn't resist the fabulous Senders for very long. Haha! Nobody ever did!

Before going on stage, Joe and Paul stopped by our dressing room to say hi—kind as always. It was a fabulous show, and we'll be forever thankful to the Clash for hiring us. I have to admit, apart from Mick Jones—who might not have been the friendliest chap—the Clash guys were pretty cool!

Bill, our guitar player, went to tour England for three weeks with some other good friends of ours: the Stray Cats, who were also starting to get really big. They decided to "fatten up" their rockabilly sound for that tour by adding a second guitar, a piano, and a sax. That same month, I went to see my family in Paris, and while I was there, I decided to go by the club Les Bains Douches with our record under my arm to see if The Senders could play there. There had been a great little article about us in the French music magazine *Rock & Folk*, entitled "PUNK BLUES!" and I thought the club might know about us.

As I walked into the club's office, I introduced myself and the band to the guy behind the desk. He had never heard of us and, at first, told me to come back in six months, but when he noticed that our record came from Max's, he asked if we had gone to New York to record it.

"No, we live there. I'm actually the only French one in the band—all the others are American. I'm a Frenchman in an American band!" And with that, he immediately offered me a solid week of shows any time we wanted. I guess it was a good idea to specify that we were from the States! That evening, I called our manager in New York to ask if he could finance Steve and Marc's airfare so we could play for a week at Les Bains Douches, but he told me to go to hell.

"I'm already in Paris and Bill is in England. All he has to do is take the ferry. My sister can put a couple of them up. We'll manage. It'll cost nothing, and we'll make ten times more playing every night at Les Bains Douches than we would in New York—not to mention this will get us known in Paris, then France, then Europe, *the entire world!*"

"But of course . . ." he drawled, sounding like he was really getting annoyed now. "I'm not buying any plane tickets for anyone—are you joking? What's next?"

"Yeah, but we don't have enough money. We're more like flat broke, and you and your partner may have organized Woodstock, but I don't think you're doing very much for us at all and if things don't change soon, I'm not even sure I'm going to re-sign the contract when it ends . . ."

"It ends now!" he yelled and slammed down the phone.

I came back to New York feeling pretty disappointed. At the airport, this big Black customs woman looked at my passport and asked me, "Musician? Are you in a rock band?"

"Yes, The Senders."

"Never heard of you!"

"Yeah, yeah, I know . . ." I felt like saying, "but if we had played for a week at Les Bains Douches then you would have . . ."

Risé and I were starting to get high more and more often, but we were careful—we were *not* junkies. We only did it once or twice a month . . . or only on weekends . . . or every three days . . . but no more!! We were hooked, and it was starting to ruin our marriage. Going down to Norfolk Street or Avenue D to buy dope was terrifying, but I was down there every two days now. . . .

You got to this abandoned ruin of a building, and after slipping through a hole in the wall, you had to walk down a hallway littered with trash. Then you had to climb upstairs in total darkness. Half the steps were broken or missing altogether, and you had to try go to up without falling in between—all the while, hoping you wouldn't get murdered. You'd get about two flights up and suddenly find yourself crashing into someone else you hadn't seen. *BAM! Shit! There's someone there!* From the second floor up, there'd be a line reaching all the way to the fifth floor. You had to wait in the dark behind a hundred other guys. Talking was forbidden, and every now and then you'd hear the dealer's security remind everybody, "Ssshhh . . . quiet down there, or no dope!" Security went up and down the stairs, wielding baseball bats.

I often waited for more than an hour, fucking terrified—like those times when there was no more dope, and I had to stay there, in silence, until the next shipment arrived. Once in the building, no one was allowed to leave unless the security said so by announcing, "Green light." If they said "red light," that meant you had to stay put. If you didn't follow their rules, they'd kill you without a second thought. Who would give a damn about another dead junkie in an abandoned building? There must have been corpses everywhere in there. Once you got to the fifth floor and it was finally your turn, you'd walk to a metal door reinforced fifteen times—like a safe in a bank—and put your money, in ten-dollar bills, through a little hole pierced in the center. You'd say "D" or "C" to specify if you wanted dope or coke, and then you waited for the little bags to come out of the same hole. Then you'd get the fuck out of there in a hurry and run down the stairs in the dark playing "Let's See If I Can Get to the Ground Floor Alive."

To give it a more official feel, they would stamp their little cellophane bags with brand names and logos, usually picking names like Magnum or Death. The dealers understood the importance of advertising. We were always saying things like, "Oh, did you try Skull on 2nd Street? It's really good this week." Seven-Up was the best brand for a while.

The worst thing was when you got to the bottom of the stairs and it was "red light." If the lookout at the corner saw a police car, no one could leave before it was clear. When that happened, you'd be stuck there, your pockets full of dope, in pitch black with an army of desperate junkies. Life was cheap by the front door. At least the guards there gave you a vague feeling of security. Where it really got bad, though, was when you got to the corner of the block—the entrance to the lion's den, Alphabet City, where it was every man for himself. The best you could do was run for your life. There, you were good for it either way you went: they could get your money on your way there, and or your dope on your way back. That's where the most dangerous and poorest Black and Puerto Rican junkies waited for their prey, their lambs . . . their little white junkies from good families, who were coming from Tribeca or the Upper West Side. The artists, the nine-to-fivers in suits who had just gotten paid, each one more lost and terrified than the other, pockets filled with money or dope. They knew damn well that the neighborhood muggers saw them as perfect victims, vulnerable to the point where they couldn't even go to the police—because they'd had their drugs stolen. It was a good idea to wear sneakers and be ready to take off in a flash. Even better, having a getaway car waiting around the corner. I saw quite a few of them get jumped right in front of me like a bunch of rabbits attacked by wild dogs, everybody taking off in all directions. I, myself, beat the hundred-meter record a few times on Avenue D. It was military maneuvers between the muggers and the cops, and getting home with what you had just bought was never a guarantee.

To avoid the "freshmen" that attracted the cops, the best dope houses catered exclusively to professional junkies, those they knew would be back every day. To get in there, you had to show "ID," which meant rolling up your sleeves to show the tracks on your arm. Every now and then, some of the dope houses would be closed without any explanation. They wouldn't even leave a sign on the door. You could easily venture into a building where there'd be no one but a couple of guys waiting to cut your throat. To avoid that, regulars would discreetly signal to each other in the street: "530 is closed. 573 across the street is open. . . ."

Sometimes, they'd all be closed, leaving you with no choice but to buy your stuff on the sidewalk from gypsy dealers, independents, guys who sold generic dope, which could easily be crushed aspirin, if you were lucky—or Ajax or rat poison if you weren't. On the sidewalks, it was the lottery, and you never really knew what you were taking home.

So, one evening, after taking off my watch and my ring, I went down to Norfolk to get four bags. I had just come out of the building and was heading toward Houston Street when this big Puerto Rican guy with a thick black mustache asked me for a light. I told him I didn't smoke and picked up my step, but I wasn't able to get away. He pushed me against the wall and took out a knife, saying, "Your dope—give me everything. Hurry up!"

"I don't have any, I swear. I'm sorry!"

"I saw you come out of the dope house—you think I'm stupid? Cough it up or I'll kill you, motherfucker," he whispered nervously, glancing around.

"All right." I was shaking like a leaf, but I took one of the four cellophane bags out of my pocket.

"The rest, hurry up! Gimme all you got. Do you wanna die? Turn your pockets inside out."

I don't know what possessed me. You have to be pretty badly hooked to justify that kind of move, but without another thought, I shoved the guy off of me and took off running as fast as I could. I'd never moved so fast in my life.

"How did it go?" Risé asked when I came back home seventeen seconds later.

"I lost one of them on the way . . . but apart from that, no problem, samo . . ."

Johnny, now without the Heartbreakers, was going to play at Irving Plaza with The Senders and the B-Girls opening up. Irving Plaza was an old ballroom from the twenties right around the block from Max's, near Gramercy Park. With its big classic room and balconies all around, it was a great place to see a band. Everything at Irving Plaza seemed old and authentic: beautiful staircases done in retro Chinese style, all red and gold and with dragons and all. I loved the atmosphere there. I'd seen a few good shows at Irving Plaza, like the Gun Club with Jeffrey Lee Pierce, the Vipers, and the

Cramps, and we'd played there three or four times. It was a blast every time.

When I arrived at sound check, I could tell there was a problem. Johnny's roadies were busy setting up a large wooden cross on which he was supposed to be crucified during the show. But the owner of Irving Plaza, who was probably religious, didn't seem to find it funny at all.

"Are you joking?" the guy was yelling furiously at the roadies onstage. "Take this thing off the stage immediately, and you can tell Mr. Thunders to go get crucified somewhere else! Where the hell do you think you are, exactly? We don't appreciate this kind of bad taste here! And tell him that if he doesn't like it, we'll cancel the whole show. And if I see that cross onstage tonight, I'll pull the plug and that will be the end of that! We like rock 'n' roll here, but we respect religion too, mister!"

Johnny showed up a little later, and the roadie told him they wouldn't have the cross.

"They can go fuck themselves!" Johnny replied, rolling his eyes and casually sitting down backstage.

"Do you wanna come eat with us?" Steve asked him.

"No, go ahead. I'm gonna hang out here a bit. See you in awhile," he said, taking a syringe out of his pocket.

When we came back around ten, the room was already packed. We went to hang out at the bar upstairs, and around eleven the B-Girls arrived. As they walked into the dressing room, they found Johnny asleep on the sofa, completely naked.

"Ooohh! He's naked!" they all shrieked together, which woke him up.

"Eehhh? What time is it?" he asked, getting up. "Where's the bathroom?"

"Down the corridor, on the left."

"No! No! On the left!" they all screamed, laughing hysterically as Johnny, high as a kite and naked as a jaybird, kept going straight and mistakenly opened the wrong door, which led directly to the room where the audience was, just to the right of the stage. "Ladies and gentlemen, *Johnny Thunders!*"

Later on, when he felt better and had gotten dressed, he went on to perform. And when the curtain came up, there he was, his guitar hanging in front of him, crucified on his cross . . . and nobody pulled no plug.

Steve was starting to complain more and more that his ears hurt after the shows, and that he was having a hard time hearing. It was rapidly getting worse and he was getting to be pretty deaf. Boxing must have fucked him up pretty badly, and the loud volume of rock 'n' roll in the clubs every night was probably not ideal.

We played the Rock Against Racism festival. We had no idea why we were headlining that big outdoor show one afternoon in Central Park—especially considering that when the guy had called to ask if we would play, Steve had replied, "Why not? We'd play against any race, man!" Also on the bill were the Invaders, Lenny

Kaye, Joy Rider, The Stilettos, Cheetah Chrome, Panic Squad, and a few others. We played in front of two thousand hippies of all races, all wearing tie-dyed T-shirts.

A few hours later, we were opening up for Crazy Cavan & the Rhythm Rockers at Max's. Kings of the British Teddy Boys and a fabulous rockabilly band, Crazy Cavan—who were unknown in New York—had brought with them about sixty authentic London Teds, complete with drapes, drains, creepers, spectacular pompadours, and tattoos everywhere. As their last visit to the States was a complete flop, they decided to bring their fans along! There were two busloads of them parked in front of Max's. Inside, it was like you were in a fucking movie. They did the whole tour like that, bringing their British retro fifties fanatics across the States with them: Nashville, Memphis, Norfolk. . . . They must have placed an ad in London to the effect of: *Teddie Boys go USA! Visit the United States and go see Crazy Cavan every night. 300 pounds all included.*

As far as rockabilly went, Robert Gordon was unbeatable in the Elvis style. His band, the Tuff Darts, were not especially interesting, though. So he left them and started another, first with Chris Spedding, then with none other than Link Wray on guitar, which was cool as fuck. We played with them a few times at Max's, as with all the other bands who formed the retro fifties–early sixties clique in the New York scene, like Mink DeVille, the Stray Cats, Levi & the Rockats, the A-Bones, the B-Girls, the Fleshtones, the Comateens, the Zantees, the Rousers, the Cramps, Buzz & the Flyers, etc.

Michael Gene, the guitarist for Buzz & the Flyers, blew his brains out. We couldn't believe it. I'd arrived at Rebop to find Risé in tears. Since he hadn't shown up for work, she called his house and learned the terrible news. It seemed that earlier that day a doctor had told him he was infected with that terrible new disease we were all suddenly hearing about: the "gay cancer," which some were starting to call by its real name, AIDS.

New York lost a *great* guitarist that day and a really cool guy.

Kevin, one of Bruce's friends, got it too, and he died in the blink of an eye. I had last seen him on St. Mark's Place, and when I saw him again at the same spot two months later, I couldn't believe what I was seeing. He looked like he had come straight out of Auschwitz. I hardly recognized him. Three weeks later, he was dead. Same thing soon after with Genaro, our friend from Provincetown. *Bam*, vanished. Then it was Brent, our friend from Boston. Then Cathy, then Chris, Michael, Michelle, Patty, Alan. . . .

Suddenly, people were dropping like flies, and panic set in. Overnight, everything changed—forever. It was simply the end of an era—an era when we were free like we never would be again.

AIDS immediately dug a huge hole in the history of New York's culture, affecting so many artists, who often were gay or drug addicts or both. All those paintings that were never painted, all those books and songs that were never written, those melodies never composed, those dances never choreographed, those movies never made. . . . It was as if AIDS was taking all the best people first, all those who had something interesting to say . . . and who never got a chance to say it.

We had to close Rebop. The rent had gotten too high. It was sad, but we had no choice. Since we still owned a large inventory of retro clothing, we rented a storage space and filled it up. We started selling our clothes at the flea market on Canal Street every weekend. On Saturday night, after a whole day at the flea market, I'd run to play with The Senders, come home around four or five in the morning, down a coffee, and run back to the flea market to make it there by six to rent the space. I looked pretty funny by Sunday night! . . . . And more than a few times, I had to go back to play yet again that night, too.

I woke up one morning—well, one afternoon—finally realizing that dope had completely taken control of my life and destroyed everything in it. My marriage with

Risé was falling apart. We fought all the time, and the only moments of peace we had together were when we were stoned, passed out somewhere in the apartment. Now there were only the stoned days and the days we were waiting to be.

How could that have happened? We didn't get it. The Senders, either.

You take heroin or you don't. There is nothing between the two. It isn't a recreational drug; it's a lifestyle. You don't take "a little" heroin, and anybody who believes you can has a bad surprise waiting for them around the corner.

Heroin is a spider, and once it gets you in its web, it has all the time in the world. It can eat you right away or it can save you for later, but without exception and with no pity at all, it will eat you.

Risé and I decided to go our separate ways.

I slept on the sofa at Cookie's Bleecker Street apartment for a couple of weeks before finding a little studio on 3rd Street by Avenue B.

What sadness. Those were perhaps the most miserable months of my life.

Things weren't much better for The Senders, unfortunately. Steve had gone completely deaf in one ear and was now wearing a hearing aid in the other. To top it off, not only were Steve, Marc, and I seriously strung out, but now so was Basile. Only Bill had never touched the stuff, and he was now locked up in the psychiatric hospital!

He'd been having dinner with friends one evening when suddenly, to everyone's surprise, he became a statue. He stopped mid-sentence, frozen. They called an ambulance. It was sort of a nervous breakdown, a motor shutdown. He hadn't slept for three days, the nut! He'd been taking some sort of bad speed or something on which he didn't need to sleep at all.

Basile was in pretty bad shape, too. He decided to go back to Oklahoma.

Marc Zermati, the French underground music producer, came to New York to have us record an album for his label Skydog. We told him that Bill was in the hospital and that it would be a while before we could record anything. Marc was nice enough to give us some time, and he went back to France for two or three months. When he returned to New York to make the record, Bill still hadn't made any improvement. They'd doped him up with barbiturates, and he was still at the hospital, totally out of it. It was *One Flew Over the Cuckoo's Nest.* I spoke with his mom on the phone almost every night; it was really sad. I would tell her that a project like a new album might do Bill some good, that he should come out of the hospital, if only to get a little fresh air. . . . But time was passing and nothing was changing. We finally got Bill out of there for a practice session for the recording, but it was a disaster. He limply shook my hand and got his guitar out of the case very slowly. He could hardly play at all and definitely didn't remember the chords of our songs. He'd look at his hand, quietly muttering, "G . . . one finger there, and A . . . like that with the other finger here. D, with that finger there . . ." We were holding back tears. He was fucking gone, even worse than us. . . . He went back to the hospital, and we went to get some dope.

He let us know through his mom that he wanted us to record the album, that we shouldn't wait for him, and that he didn't want us to quit because of him. . . .

We made some tapes for Marc Zermati in a studio in Times Square with Barry Ryan, the Rockats' guitar player, filling in. But we were utterly demoralized . . . and completely strung out.

And then came the final blow. The doctor told Steve that he should learn sign language as soon as possible, because he was going to be totally deaf within a year. The doctor said the damage was irreversible, even if he stayed away from noise. Poor Steve, it was horrible. But the boxer took it with an impressive grace, smiling through it all.

So all that was left of The Senders was one deaf guy, one in a nuthouse, and two at the dope house. . . . There wasn't much else to do other than call it a day.

We played our last show at the Peppermint Lounge with Barry Ryan and Wayne Kramer on guitars and Danny Ray on saxophone. Before going onstage, Steve told us, "Whatever you do, don't change the song's arrangement, because I can't hear you. Just follow me and we'll manage."

It was a pretty good show anyway and the room was packed.

Thank you, thank you. See you real soon. Goodnight, everybody.

I started working as a printer for a company that did mail surveys.

I printed their questionnaires from nine to five, and then I went home. My place was only a block away from the dope house, and I could get my dose—which had become daily—in five minutes.

I hadn't been living on 3rd Street very long when one night, around midnight, I shot up and OD'd immediately. By some miracle, I woke up. I pulled the syringe out of my arm and I looked at the clock. Shit! It was one in the morning—I'd been out for almost an hour. I pulled myself out of bed, noticing that all my muscles ached. Then I caught a glimpse of myself in the mirror and I couldn't believe what I saw. I looked like I belonged in *Night of the Living Dead*. I'd gone completely gray, my lips were blue and badly cracked, and I had two black eyes.

I knew right away that it must have taken me longer than an hour to get to that point. I jerked the curtains open, and the sun splashed the room with light. It was one in the afternoon, not one in the morning. I had been unconscious with a syringe in my arm, alone at home, for more than twelve hours. . . . I started to cry.

This time I'd nearly done it. I could just as well have never woken up.

It was more than a miracle. It scared me enough that I was forced to accept reality and look at things as they were.

I sat there for a long time.

There was nothing left. No more Risé, no more Senders, no more Rebop. . . . And it was also painfully obvious that I wasn't going to be lucky enough to wake up after a twelve-hour overdose too many more times. . . . Yet, I was already thinking of buying some more! I was going to die all alone in here if I didn't do something quick. I needed help. I was too ashamed to go to my family, which was stupid because I know they would have helped me faster than anyone.

Fortunately, I still had a few good friends left who weren't junkies. Bill Moser came to mind right away.

Bill was a former bouncer at Kenny's Castaways and had been a part-time roadie for The Senders. He was unbelievably nice, but he was also one huge mother-fucker. He stood over six feet tall and was terrific at basketball. He'd obviously had no problem finding work as a bouncer. His presence alone would stop any fight on the spot. He was a gentle giant. Since I didn't own a gun, I figured that if he blocked my way, I simply wouldn't be able to go cop. I knew that was what I needed: to be physically restrained, to be tied to a chair.

I grabbed the phone before I could change my mind and dialed his number. I told him what had happened and simply asked if he could maybe stay with me a bit, because I wanted to quit but didn't trust myself anymore.

"Hey, it just so happens that I don't allow good rhythm and blues singers to die!" he answered me, laughing, before adding, "I'm sorry, but since you're asking me so nicely, it is, from this moment on, my full responsibility to make sure you don't even think of going to buy that shit. . . . Or hurry the fuck up, 'cause I'm coming over right now. You see? Now you got a problem, Phil! Hahaha!! See you in a minute."

Indeed, he got there five minutes later, yelling, "Your syringe! Where is it? Hand it over! In the trash!"

Bill seemed happy to put himself between me and the dope house. He stayed with me in my little apartment for almost a week. He lived with three roommates anyway, so he didn't mind spending a few days over at my place. If things weren't going too well, we'd smoke a joint but for the most part we managed.

Sometimes I would tell him I was feeling better, that he could go home, and every time he would roll his eyes. "You think I'm stupid?"

He followed me everywhere. I hardly had the right to go to the bathroom on my own. We went to the supermarket together. We looked like lovers.

I didn't sleep for several nights. You know the score: every muscle aches, it's kind of unpleasant. . . . I had terrible nightmares. Every half hour, I would wake up shivering in a cold sweat, my legs crushed by the blanket—turn to the left, turn to the right, kick my feet a few times in the air, growl, fall asleep again, have a few more nightmares. I'd be onstage with The Senders, the microphone didn't work, I had no voice left, people were starting to boo us, laughing cruelly. . . . I'd wake up screaming, delirious with fever. I was thirsty, throwing up, had the runs, terrible headaches, pain in my shoulders, in my arms, cramps everywhere. . . . I was more miserable than if I had the worst flu.

Bill Moser snored peacefully on a mattress in front of the door.

There was also a terrible grumpiness that came in heavy waves, but I couldn't get too aggressive with Bill—he could break my nose. I was forced to stay as polite as I could, and that kept me from completely losing it.

Finally, I slept for two days. Bill had me call my job to say that I had a bad cold and after giving up a week of sick leave to go "cold turkey," I went back to work. He would drop me off and pick me up. After that, he put me on "probation" for a little while. He had a key made without even asking, and told me that he was going to frequently drop by without any notice, just to see the size of my pupils. If they seemed too small for his taste, he would simply beat the crap out of me.

"No point changing the lock, either. I'd have no problem knocking the door down!"

But more than that, I didn't want to disappoint him. He'd been so cool, and that's what helped me the most. I had already let myself down, but I hadn't yet disappointed him, and I wanted it to stay that way—and that alone was giving me strength.

Little by little, knowing that he was always keeping an eye on me, I started to move on and think of other things.

So that was it, then. Had I finally won that fight for good?

No. Not quite. Unfortunately, there was still one more round to go.

Two months later, I thought I was far from all that, but then temptation came back full blast. One night, I started falling back into the old trap: "Only one time, I promise, it's cool. . . ."

Five minutes later, I was walking back up 2nd Street with two bags of heroin in my hand, ashamed of myself.

And then, just like I was James Stewart in *It's a Wonderful Life*, an angel appeared—only this time in the form of a big Puerto Rican with a gun. He took me by surprise, sneaking up behind me and grabbing me by my coat, he pressed a gun into my stomach. I quickly gave him my dope, whispering, almost in tears, "It's all I've got, I swear."

He gave me a disgusted look and said, "Faggot!" before letting go of me and casually sauntering away with my dope.

I broke into a thousand pieces on the sidewalk, like a crystal vase, in slow motion.

That time was my last, I can—fortunately—say, thirty-five years later.

I went home and smashed everything: the dishes, the records (well, maybe not the records!), the furniture. . . . I lost it.

Since I'd just had the heroin in my hand, I could *almost* taste it. In an instant, I *had* awoken that horrible beast inside of me and it was unbearable. I had to have some *right away*—now! I didn't have a cent left, and my nerves were all catching on fire. "Oh, no—not that nightmare, anything but that, no, no, no!" I screamed, freaking out, throwing everything I touched across the room: the stereo, the TV. . . . Nothing was spared. It didn't really matter. I didn't have anything of real value. When you're a junkie you never have much. . . .

Stupidly, I had also managed to cut the inside of my hand pretty bad, after smashing a bottle of vodka against the wall.

Actually, it was the "Faggot!" that had pushed me over the edge. The guy had just mugged me at gun-point—wasn't that enough? Did he really have to add that? I'm sure I'd been called a "faggot" many times before, and I'm sure I never gave a fuck, but this time it was the time and the place, the contempt, the spit in my face, the smirk that screamed, *You can't do anything, you pathetic junkie, 'cause you belong to me.*

That was the final straw, because I knew he was right. With my whole place in ruins, I finally fell asleep on the floor—crying, exhausted, rolled up in a ball, blood gushing from my hand.

It was over. I was cured.

My two months without dope had already given me back so much of my spirit and self-esteem, and now I was lying there, covered with shit and stinking of shame.

I had finally learned my lesson.

I don't know why I had the incredible good fortune of getting mugged that night of all nights, but I owe the guy my life, that's for sure—even more than to Bill Moser. If I had been able to get high that night, I would certainly have gone back a second time, then a third. . . . And if he hadn't called me a "faggot" like that, to top it off, I'd probably be long dead. The look in his eyes had pierced right through me, frustrating me enough to give me the strength necessary to finally hate this miserable drug and everything that went with it.

Fuck that!

. . .

It was a beautiful sunny afternoon, and I was strolling down Avenue A. Things were starting to look up: I was rediscovering the joys of buying things other than dope and had gotten myself a new electric guitar, marimbas, records. . . .

I was just starting my new project: The Backbones. Sort of a rock soul band, with only guys that weren't drugging, including Danny Ray and Brett Wilder, and Kenny Margolis from Mink DeVille. And I had just met Maggie. . . .

Bums were always putting on little improvised flea markets on Avenue A on Sundays. You'd never find much there—it was mostly homeless guys and junkies selling stuff they'd found in the trash.

One of them had a display of records on an old sheet on the ground.

As I passed by, something caught my eye: he had The Senders at Max's record, *The Seven Song Super Single* in all its splendor, with its magnificent black-and-white cover.

Surprised, I leaned over to look at it, and noticed that the guy had put a little orange tag on it that read: $1.

"One dollar!" he announced to me. "Great record—do you know this one? One dollar!"

"Yeah, I know this one!" I answered, laughing. "I was actually in this band. That's me, right there on the cover!"

He looked at me then at the picture and said, "Wow! You're right, it is you! Cool, man! I love that record, you know . . . it's just that I'm real broke right now . . ."

I smiled, winked at him, and went on my way.

"Hey, man, wait a minute, can you sign it?" he called after me, handing me the album and a marker.

I quickly wrote *Senders Forever, Phil Marcade* across the cover and gave it back to him.

I passed by his stand again a couple of hours later on my way home and I noticed that the record was still there on the sidewalk but now with my signature and a new little tag on which he had written: $1.50.

Hahaha!!

EPILOGUE

BRUCE STOPPED TAKING DRUGS AND HAS been living with AIDS for more than twenty years. He is now a high school history teacher.

Steve worked for years as a drug awareness counselor at a center for deaf juvenile delinquents. Then, in 2010, a true miracle happened: thanks to recent progress in medical science, he had, a tiny state-of-the-art electronic device implanted in his one of his ears, and after more than twenty years living in complete silence, Steve can hear again. Probably better then most of us!

Risé remarried and has a daughter.

As for me, I recorded an album and did several tours with the Backbones, playing in California a couple of times.

Then, in 1989, I decided to stop the music for a while to concentrate on painting. This hiatus lasted only a week, because I got a phone call from Midnight Records—an independent record company here in New York—asking if I would be interested in putting The Senders back together to record a Christmas song for a compilation.

"I don't know, I could call them. . . ." I said. "It's been awhile."

In the blink of an eye, I found myself in a recording studio with Bill, who was back to himself 100 percent. He was in top shape and playing guitar better than ever; he'd just gotten back from spending the last couple of years touring with the British band Savoy Brown.

Marc was there too, totally sober and off drugs.

Steve was replaced by Ritchie Lure, Walter's little brother.

It was so cool to be together again, after six years, that we decided to do a show—just one—at CBGB . . . *and off we went for another thirteen years!!!* During this time, we were going to be more successful than ever, with constant shows all over New York. We launched the club Continental Divide and put out four new records: *Do The Sender Thing (Live at CBGB), Back To Sender (Revisited), Goodbye Cruel World,* and *Outrageous & Contagious.*

Sadly, Cookie died of AIDS in 1989.

Then, Johnny and Jerry died one after the other in 1991 and 1992.

We also lost Marc along the way, when he stupidly got back into drugs in '93 and left the band. He was replaced by Ned Brewster of the Action Swingers, with whom we played as far away as Paris in 1995.

Marc died of a heroin overdose in 1997, then Ritchie died of a stroke a few months later.

Those two were like my brothers, and I miss them bitterly.

In 2000, The Senders were hailed as the "Best Bar Band in New York" by the *New York Press* in their "Best of Manhattan" issue. The article called us a "New York legend going back to the days of Max's" and ended with the words: "Definitely the Best Bar Band in New York but maybe also in the entire world!"

See! I told you!

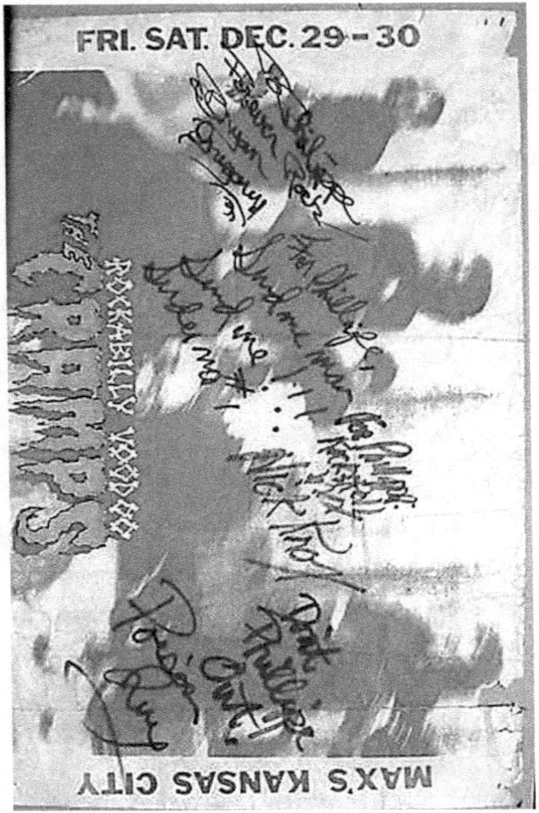

FRI. SAT. DEC. 29 – 30
ROCKABILLY VOODOO
THE CRAMPS
MAX'S KANSAS CITY

THE OTHER CHARACTERS

David Armstrong: *Photographer*

Marc Bourset: *Musician, drummer of The Senders*

Lee Brilleaux: *Musician, singer of Dr. Feelgood*

Glen Buxton: *Musician, guitarist of Alice Cooper*

Clem Burke: *Musician, drummer of Blondie*

James Chance: *Musician, saxophonist, singer of the Contortions*

Leee Black Childers: *Photographer, manager of the Heartbreakers, Levi & the Rockats*

Wayne County: *Musician, singer of the Electric Chairs*

Peter Crowley: *Manager of Max's Kansas City*

Jimmy Destri: *Musician, keyboard player of Blondie*

Willy DeVille: *Musician, singer of Mink DeVille*

Levi Dexter: *Musician, singer of Levi & the Rockats*

Divine: *Actor, drag icon*

John Felice: *Musician, singer of the Real Kids*

Michael Gene: *Musician, guitarist of Buzz & the Flyers*

Nan Goldin: *Photographer*

Robert Gordon: *Musician, singer of the Tuff Darts*

Debbie Harry: *Musician, singer of Blondie*

Richard Hell: *Musician, bass player, singer of the Heartbreakers and the Voidoids.*

Lux Interior: *Musician, singer of the Cramps*

Poison Ivy: *Musician, guitarist of the Cramps*

Wilko Johnson: *Musician, guitarist of Dr. Feelgood*

Mick Jones: *Musician, guitarist of the Clash*

Joseph: *Monkey*

Arthur Kane: *Musician, bass player of the New York Dolls*

Wayne Kramer: *Musician, guitarist of MC5 and Gang War*

Hilly Kristal: *Owner of CBGB and manager of the Dead Boys*

Lalo: *Roadie for The Senders*

Neon Leon: *Musician, singer of the Rainbow Express*

Walter Lure: *Musician, guitarist of the Heartbreakers*

Tony Machine: *Musician, drummer of the New York Dolls, The Senders, and Buster Poindexter*

Madonna: *Next-door neighbor at Music Building*

Legs McNeil*: Creator of* Punk magazine

Bob Marley: *Musician, singer of the Wailers*

Bill Moser: *Bouncer at Kenny's Castaways, roadie for The Senders*

Cookie Mueller: *Actress, author*

Jorge Navarro: *Musician, guitarist of The Senders*

Basile Nodow: *Musician, guitarist of The Senders*

Jerry Nolan: *Musician, drummer of the New York Dolls and the Heartbreakers*

Octavio: *Musician, guitarist, next-door neighbor*

Jeffrey Lee Pierce: *Musician, singer of the Gun Club*

Dee Dee Ramone: *Musician, bass player of the Ramones*

Joey Ramone: *Musician, singer of the Ramones*

Johnny Ramone: *Musician, guitarist of the Ramones*

Tommy Ramone: *Musician, drummer of the Ramones*

Billy Rath: *Musician, bass player of the Heartbreakers*

Danny Ray: *Musician, saxophonist of The Senders and the Backbones*

Laurie "Reedy" Reid: *Musician, guitarist of The Senders*

Billy Roger: *Musician, drummer of The Senders*

Johnny Rotten: *Musician, singer of the Sex Pistols*

Steve Shevlin: *Musician, bass player of The Senders*

Paul Simonon: *Musician, bass player of the Clash*

Nancy Spungen: *Girlfriend of Sid Vicious*

Sable Starr: *Girlfriend of Johnny Thunders*

Chris Stein: *Musician, guitarist of Blondie*

Ty Stix: *Musician, drummer of The Senders*

Joe Strummer: *Musician, singer/guitarist of the Clash*

Wild Bill Thompson: *Musician, guitarist of The Senders*

Johnny Thunders: *Musician, singer/guitarist of the New York Dolls, the Heartbreakers, Gang War*

Toots: *Girlfriend of Willy DeVille*

Gary Valentine: *Musician, bass player of Blondie*

Arturo Vega: *Artist, friend of the Ramones*

Sid Vicious: *Musician, bass player of the Sex Pistols*

Andy Warhol: *Artist*

John Waters: *Movie director, author*

Marc Zermati: *Producer (Skydog Records)*

Mikey Zone: *Musician, guitarist of the Fast*

Paul Zone: *Musician, singer of the Fast*

Phil, Walter Lure, Mary, Max, Sharon, Cookie, Bruce, Risé, Pam, Kevin, and Cathy outside Rebop, 1978

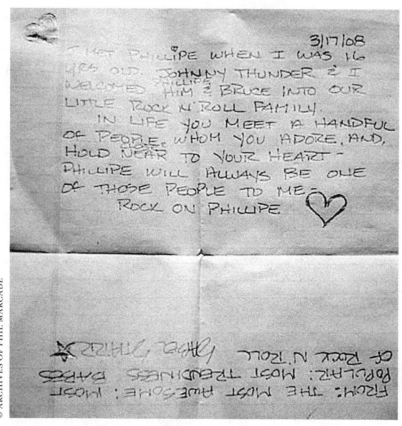

Note to the author from Sable Starr (1957–2009)

When she wrote me this note in 2008, I told her, "Ah, so your name is spelled Sabel, not Sable, as you are generally referred to. I've been wondering for years. You have finally solved this mystery." She answered me "I don't know either!!! I change it all the time, I can't decide!!" Haha!! I miss her. —*P.M.*

Special thanks to
Pierre Marcadé, Phyllis Stein, Janet Rosen, Carly Sommerstein,
Amber Sexton, Legs McNeil, Debbie Harry,
and Sable Starr.

ABOUT THE AUTHOR

PHIL MARCADE LEFT PARIS IN HIS late teens to begin "a few months" of travel that would lead to a forty-year-stay in the US, mostly in New York City. He was at the center of the origins of the punk rock explosion, as a musician (founder and lead singer of The Senders) and insider, forming intimate friendships with artists and muscians including Johnny Thunders, Nan Goldin, Cookie Mueller, Wayne Kramer, Debbie Harry, Nancy Spungen, and Willie DeVille. In addition to writing, he works as a painter and graphic artist. He lives in Italy.

Recent and Forthcoming Books from Three Rooms Press

FICTION

Meagan Brothers
Weird Girl and What's His Name

Ron Dakron
Hello Devilfish!

Michael T. Fournier
Hidden Wheel
Swing State

Janet Hamill
Tales from the Eternal Café
(Introduction by Patti Smith)

William Least Heat-Moon
Celestial Mechanics

Eamon Loingsigh
Light of the Diddicoy
Exile on Bridge Street

John Marshall
The Greenfather

Aram Saroyan
Still Night in L.A.

Richard Vetere
The Writers Afterlife
Champagne and Cocaine

MEMOIR & BIOGRAPHY

Nassrine Azimi and
Michel Wasserman
Last Boat to Yokohama:
The Life and Legacy of
Beate Sirota Gordon

James Carr
BAD: The Autobiography of
James Carr

Richard Katrovas
Raising Girls in Bohemia:
Meditations of an American Father;
A Memoir in Essays

Judith Malina
Full Moon Stages:
Personal Notes from
50 Years of The Living Theatre

Phil Marcade
Punk Avenue:
Inside the New York City
Underground, 1972-1982

Stephen Spotte
My Watery Self:
Memoirs of a Marine Scientist

PHOTOGRAPHY-MEMOIR

Mike Watt
On & Off Bass

SHORT STORY ANTHOLOGIES

Dark City Lights: New York Stories
edited by Lawrence Block

Have a NYC I, II & III:
New York Short Stories;
edited by Peter Carlaftes
& Kat Georges

Crime + Music: The Sounds of Noir
edited by Jim Fusilli

Songs of My Selfie:
An Anthology of Millennial Stories
edited by Constance Renfrow

This Way to the End Times:
Classic and New Stories of
the Apocalypse
edited by Robert Silverberg

MIXED MEDIA

John S. Paul
Sign Language: A Painter's
Notebook (photography, poetry
and prose)

TRANSLATIONS

Thomas Bernhard
On Earth and in Hell
(poems of Thomas Bernhard
with English translations by
Peter Waugh)

Patrizia Gattaceca
Isula d'Anima / Soul Island
(poems by the author
in Corsican with English
translations)

César Vallejo | Gerard Malanga
Malanga Chasing Vallejo
(selected poems of César Vallejo
with English translations
and additional notes by
Gerard Malanga)

George Wallace
EOS: Abductor of Men
(selected poems of George
Wallace with Greek translations)

HUMOR

Peter Carlaftes
A Year on Facebook

DADA

Maintenant: A Journal of
Contemporary Dada Writing & Art
(Annual, since 2008)

FILM & PLAYS

Israel Horovitz
My Old Lady: Complete Stage Play
and Screenplay with an Essay on
Adaptation

Peter Carlaftes
Triumph For Rent (3 Plays)
Teatrophy (3 More Plays)

Kat Georges
Three Somebodies: Plays about
Notorious Dissidents

POETRY COLLECTIONS

Hala Alyan
Atrium

Peter Carlaftes
DrunkYard Dog
I Fold with the Hand I Was Dealt

Thomas Fucaloro
It Starts from the Belly and Blooms

Inheriting Craziness is Like
a Soft Halo of Light

Kat Georges
Our Lady of the Hunger

Robert Gibbons
Close to the Tree

Israel Horovitz
Heaven and Other Poems

David Lawton
Sharp Blue Stream

Jane LeCroy
Signature Play

Philip Meersman
This is Belgian Chocolate

Jane Ormerod
Recreational Vehicles on Fire
Welcome to the Museum of Cattle

Lisa Panepinto
On This Borrowed Bike

George Wallace
Poppin' Johnny

Three Rooms Press | New York, NY | Current Catalog: www.threeroomspress.com
Three Rooms Press books are distributed by PGW/Ingram: www.pgw.com